Kathleen Dayus was born in Hockley. In her first book of autobiography, *Her People* (1982), she vividly recalled the story of her Edwardian childhood, growing up in the slums. It won her enormous popular and critical acclaim, and the 1983 J. R. Ackerly Prize for autobiography. *Where There's Life* (1985) and *All My Days* (1988) continued her story through adolescence, as a young munitions worker during the First World War, marriage and life below the poverty line in the 1920s. Early widowhood and the Depression forced her to relinquish her children to Dr Barnardo's homes until, eight long years later, she could make a home for them again.

In *The Best of Times*, Kathleen Dayus brings us more life stories. Her extraordinary memory for the sights, sounds and smells of her youth, her marvellous sense of the comic and above all her spirited refusal to do anything but live life to the full, deservedly make her one of the most compelling and best-loved storytellers of our time.

Now in her late 80s, Kathleen Dayus lives in Birmingham still and has twelve grandchildren and eight great-grandchildren.

*Also published by Virago*

*Her People*
*All My Days*
*Where There's Life*

# Kathleen Dayus

# THE BEST OF TIMES

Published by VIRAGO PRESS Limited 1991
20–23 Mandela Street, Camden Town,
London NW1 0HQ

Typeset by CentraCet, Cambridge
Printed and bound in Great Britain by
Cox & Wyman Ltd, Reading, Berkshire

# Contents

To my loving, caring
daughter Jean and her
husband Sam Rainey

# An Almost Forgotten Era

I believe today that many memories die hard, whether they are good, bad or indifferent. But as for me, I can never forget those bug-infested back-to-back hovels where I was born in 1903 and lived twenty-nine years in poverty and hardship, until I made heartbreaking decisions to leave all this behind me and to begin a new life for the better, for myself and my young family.

Often today, in my late years, I still find myself wandering around these old haunts, around the Jewellery Quarter, and recalling those once cobbled horse-roads and back alleyways, where I used to run to school with bare feet, in rags, with many other poor half-starved kids, begging for food outside factory gates. Many parents had no time to give us love or affection, which we needed, only strong discipline with the bamboo cane at the ready. Many times, too, old Vicar Smith would chase us with his walking-stick if he caught us playing in the churchyard of St Paul's Church, which we named 'Titty-bottle Park'.

And as I stroll along today, I notice how bright and clean this church and the surrounding district are. There are no more of those dilapidated back-to-back hovels where, I remember, people often begged and scratched for a crust of bread. Today you can see lovely flats and restaurants, where people live and dine in comfort, yet many of these surrounding buildings have only had a facelift. Also, many famous landmarks have gone now to make way for progress – but let us not forget our history, and who we are. Yet as I stroll around St Paul's Square and down George Street, I notice that the King Edward pub is still there, reminding me of the time I used to follow the hurdy-gurdy man around the square and along the 'Parade'. Many of us kids, when we came out of school, would hide up an entry and dance to the tunes he played, with our ragged frocks well above our knees.

Newhall Street had many little shops then. There was one shop I still remember well, where I used to fetch Mum's faggots and peas and dip my finger in, but not enough for Mum to notice. Once, she smelt my breath and I had the cane. But I didn't give her another chance – I always put my mouth under the tap in the yard before I took the basin in. But one day she sent me for a pint of milk. I knew she wouldn't be able to smell that, so after having a drink I added a drop of water, just about a tablespoon. As soon as I got indoors she asked, ''Ave yer bin drinkin' any?'

'No, Mum,' I lied, as I began to tremble inside.

(But you could never lie to or deceive my mother.)

'Are yer sure?' she asked again, staring hard at me.

When I shook my head and replied no again, I felt my face colour up. She pulled me towards her and cried out, 'Well, if yer tellin' me the truth, let's see yer spit!'

As soon as I spat, she could tell I'd lied. I had that bamboo cane across my bare bum five times, and was sent to bed without my nightly cocoa.

Newhall Street was famous for cheap food. The shops sold almost everything: cow heels, tripe, chitterlings, pigs' trotters – you name them, they sold them, all piping hot. Leaving the shops that once were behind, I walk along Legge Lane, where I come to the old Camden Drive School, which I attended with my brother and sisters eighty-three years ago. I was then five years old. Yet many of these old buildings have now been renovated and turned into offices and workshops.

I recall the stories my granny used to tell me: how this district was always called the Jewellery Quarter. Many people with large families – like my mother and father, and their families – who once lived in these hovels had no prospects, just living from hand to mouth, and many who could not afford their rent let off their living-room to people who wanted to start a small business. They themselves moved to the upper floor to live. But Granny said as soon as the landlords or the agents found out, they raised the rent to a level they knew the tenants couldn't afford. So they were either turned out into the street or sent into the workhouse. This left the entire old houses to be let or sold to people who wanted to start up making jewellery. From then on, it grew to be what is still called the Jewellery Quarter today. There are still many alterations to be done to these buildings, yet many have only had a coat of paint and a facelift. There are still the back yards, brewhouses, and even old brick sheds where people used to keep pigeons, and did their washing ready for the pawnshops, yet people still ply their trades there.

As I walk on down the cobbled alleyway Camden Drive, where I was born, I am surprised to see the school wall and its playground, still just as Hitler's bombs left it. That was in the heavy raids on Birmingham in April 1941. Alongside the school wall, also, are to be seen the ruins of the iron foundry where my two eldest brothers once worked.

A lump comes to my throat as I think how sad and neglected and forgotten this place is today – just as we people were, who lived down that narrow cobbled alley many, many years ago.

It was a sad time for all of us that night the bombs came without warning.

Many of us lost loved ones, some to be buried in a communal grave in Warstone Lane Cemetery, just a few yards from where we once lived. This cemetery is neglected too, and I hope that one day it will have a facelift, to remind us not to forget our loved ones.

Just a few more yards I walk, and I come to the junction of Warstone Lane, Vyse Street and Frederic Street, where one of our famous landmarks, 'Joseph Chamberlain's Clock', stood with its ironwork painted dark green and gold, all faded and rusty. It has now been removed to be repaired and have a facelift too, but I'm told it will soon be restored to its original place. As I stand on the corner and look at that empty space, I remember the day my mother told me that when I was twelve months old she carried me to see that clock – which was erected in 1903, the year I was born – and to hear its chimes. Also, I think of the times when many of us kids leaving school at twelve midday would take it in turns to play around that monument, and look out for the Lodge Road tram making its way up to Warstone Lane, past the cemetery, round the clock, down Frederic Street, down Newhall Hill, and to the town terminus, and back again. That ride cost one penny. But today there are no trams, only buses, and you wouldn't get that same ride for less than £1.

Many years ago, I asked my teacher why the trams had holes in their slatted seats. She said they were for bugs, fleas and lice to drop through off dirty people.

As I stroll towards the city centre, near the Council House in Colemore Row, I notice that the statue of Queen Victoria is still there. Yet I can't understand why her son's statue is no longer standing beside her. I ask several people what has become of King Edward's statue – or Nelson's Column, which once stood in the Bull Ring, and many more famous statues – yet no one seems to know, or isn't interested any more.

Yet the fountain is still in the same place. That too has had a facelift, and as I stand and gaze up at it I think of the happy times we children had, dabbling our dirty sore feet in that cool, clear water. We weren't fussy, either, about having a drink afterwards. But we kept our eyes peeled for the 'bobby' coming along.

Often we had to make our own fun and games, which cost nothing, for our parents couldn't afford to buy us toys; we gave them every farthing or penny that was given to us or begged for. But we had many happy times sharing what other bits and pieces we had given us.

There was the loan of a whip and top; we'd spin it with one of Dad's borrowed leather bootlaces from his hobnail boots, or a skipping rope made from a discarded old clothes-line; sometimes if neighbours were in a good mood they'd skip with us. We also played hopscotch, making the beds from pieces of slate that fell off the roof, or we drew with a piece of chalk if we were lucky enough to take a piece from the blackboard while teacher wasn't looking. And we girls made up many, many more games.

The boys would never be seen playing with the girls – they'd be called 'sissies', which often ended up in a fight. The boys found other games to play – sometimes they'd sort the ashcans over to find a Nestlé's milk tin, knock some holes in the side and tie a piece of string round it. When washdays came round they'd hide up the entry, then as soon as they saw a neighbour leave the brewhouse quickly they'd dash in, poke a few hot embers into the tin, then run off swinging it round and round their heads to keep warm.

'Tip Cat' was another game, but this seemed to fade out, as the lads got many a belting for breaking windows. Another game I remember them playing was football, but as they couldn't afford to buy a ball they would sneak into the dry closets, tear the newspaper (we called it bum paper) off the backs of the doors, soak it well, and when it was rolled into a hard ball tied with string, this was their football.

Often there was no more bum paper for people, so when they were caught short they took their own with them. Therefore the lads would search in other people's closets, or go to the rag-and-bone yard and beg for pieces of old strips of rag or cotton waste.

It cost us kids nothing to keep happy in those days. Yet I believe we were happier than kids today, who only have to ask and get everything: too much, too soon.

During the hot summer days we would dig up hot pitch beneath the cobblestones or the wooden blocks between the tramlines, roll it into balls and play five stones (jack stones they were often called).

Some of the worst times were our punishments with the cane, but we were used to the cane and expected it. But we never learnt our lesson; we were as bad as ever when the pitch wore off our hands.

There are many reasons why I like to stroll down Memory Lane: hoping to see some of the old haunts I used to visit, hoping also that I might meet some of the people I grew up with who still remember those days and the streets where we used to linger, thinking about our tomorrows and what they might bring.

One hot summer's day, during my travels, I found myself in Great Hampton Street, and as I came to Snape's the chemist's (that was) I stood looking up at the old sign hanging from its rusty hinges. I remembered that when I was about fifteen, and thinking of the boys I used to flirt with, I often used to call in and ask Mr Snape for a penny box of carmine, a twopenny box of Phul-Nana or Shem-el-Nisim face powder, and a threepenny tablet of Erasmic soap. And for each sixpence you spent he would give you a scented card. This was to push down between your breasts to make you smell nice. But I had only small titties then, if any at all, so I used to tear the scented card into two pieces and slip them down each leg of my drawers – or passion-killers, the boys used to call them, because they had elastic round the bottoms.

Many a time, when I couldn't afford to buy these so-called luxuries, I used to lift one of Mum's pictures from the wall, spit on my fingers and rub one of the red roses from the wallpaper into my cheeks and lips.

As I walked along, I came to Hockley Street. I was now very thirsty. I knew there used to be a little café once, but it was no longer there. I looked around for somewhere to have a cup of tea, then I decided to go into the Jeweller's Arms pub and a have a shandy.

This pub is still there today, on the corner of Hockley Steet and Spencer Street, facing the small factory where I first started my enamelling business in 1931. It was crowded with young men and women factory workers having their lunch break.

The noise was deafening from the customers' chatter above the noise from the jukebox. But I managed to find my way to the bar, and while I ordered my pint of shandy I saw two elderly men staring across at me. I found a seat and ignored them. As they smiled across at me for the second time, I heard one of them call above the noise, 'You go over an' ask her, Harry.'

I felt everybody's eyes were now on me. My first thoughts were did they think I was a pick-up? Surely not – I was far too old; but you never know in this day and age!

I didn't wait to find out. I drank the rest of my shandy and left hurriedly.

I got only halfway down the street when I noticed they were close behind me. Quickly I turned round and asked why they were following me. All at once the taller one said, 'Excuse me, but we believe we know you.'

'But I don't know who *you* both are, and if you follow me any further, I shall call that policeman standing over there!' I replied angrily, pointing across the street.

Suddenly they both began to smile, so I cried, 'Well, if you say you know me, I'd be pleased to hear what you have to say!'

'We're sorry to have upset you, dear, but we want to know if your name is Mrs Flood, that used to live down Camden Drive.'

'Yes,' I replied. 'I'm the same woman that lived there, but who are you?'

'Don't you remember us? When we lived in the end house in your same yard?'

I couldn't believe my eyes, and as I stood staring up and down at these two well-dressed men, the taller one said, 'We're Harry and Joe Taylor, the twins you used to look after for me mum, when we all went hop-picking.'

'Well, well, I would never have known you. You're both grown-up, and handsome too. The last time I saw you, you were both trying to sell fishboxes for firewood in a basket carriage. That must have been before the war.'

'We done better than that, Kate . . . er, Mrs Flood . . .'

'You can call me Kate,' I replied, smiling up at him, for they were two handsome, well-dressed men – nothing like the twins I knew when I was a young woman. 'Wonderful to meet you, and how you been doing?' I asked.

'We saved every farthin' we earned and later we bought an old horse and cart off Kinver, you remember old Skinflint

Kinver, Kate, the one who kept the old stinking stables at the end of Camden Street.'

'Yes, Joe,' I replied. 'That must be the one who lent my granny the nag and cart when she left our house.'

'Kate,' Harry said, 'would you mind coming back to have a drink with us – we've only half an hour to spare and there's lots we'd like to talk about.'

'I don't think I'd like to go back there, everybody will stare and get the wrong impression, if yer know what I mean,' I replied, smiling.

'I see what yer mean; we'll go in the smoke room, where it's quieter,' Harry replied as he grinned and squeezed my hand.

How very happy I felt that day when we sat together in that smoke room!

Joe bought me a milk stout and Harry and Joe had a pint of mild and bitter each, and while we were drinking they asked if I would like a cigarette.

'I'm trying to give them up, but I'll have one today.'

'Where are you living now, Kate, not still around this old district?' Joe asked.

'No, Joe, I'm living in Handsworth with my family; you must come and visit us sometime.'

'Thank you, Kate, but I don't know when it will be. You see, we travel a lot.'

'Yes,' Harry replied. 'But we'll keep in touch.'

'What do you do, if you don't mind me asking?' I said.

'We travel the markets, Kate, going from town to town, and we're doing well. But we're honest,' they both replied, grinning at me.

'I'm pleased to hear you're both doing well, and I hope you'll always be honest. Anyhow, both, it's better than chopping up fishboxes and trying to sell them for firewood.'

'We dain't do too bad at that. We saved our little nest egg an' put it in the post office savings bank, and left it there when me and me brother went into the army. So when we was demobbed we had a few quid to start us off.'

'I'm so happy for you both,' I replied. 'But may I give you

both a word of advice? Never be ashamed of your past, or who you are, or where you come from,' I added.

'We'll *never* be that, Kate. My mum always used to tell us that. And how kind you was to us, before she died in the bombing.'

'It was sad, too,' Joe replied, 'to come back from the war to hear our neighbours and your mum and sister was killed that same night.'

'Let's change the subject,' Harry replied, looking rather sad. 'What brings you around this district, Kate?' he added.

'I like to take a stroll around these old places where we were dragged up and to reminisce, hoping to find some of the people I used to know around this district, and you're the first two I've been happy to meet. You see,' I added, 'the reason for this is, I've written three books about the story of my life, and about the people who tried to exist in those days, and now I'm giving talks to schoolchildren and elderly people in homes and community centres, hoping to meet someone I know.'

'Have you mentioned *us* in your books, Kate?' they asked, like a couple of excited kids.

'I sure have, there's pages of you and all the people who lived in that bughole Camden Drive. *And* when we all went hop-picking – you were both only about three or four years old then – and I remember at my sister's wedding, you got lost and we found you in the brewhouse copper, draining the empty whisky bottles.'

Suddenly they burst out laughing. 'We don't remember that. Was we drunk?'

'I don't know about you being drunk,' I smiled, 'but you was too tiddly to be lifted out, until I called me dad.'

'But we do remember, don't we, Joe,' Harry replied, 'when our mum told us, before we went in the army, that your brother Jack stole a pig from the hop field and how your mum won her black eye.'

'Is that in the books, too?' Joe asked.

'Yes, Joe,' I replied. 'It's all there in black and white. There's photos, too, of the families and where we lived, and all the kids in the back yards.'

'What are they called?'

'The first one with the photos in is called *Her People*. The second one is called *Where There's Life*, and the third one is called *All My Days*.'

'We sure will get them, Harry,' said Joe. 'I'm sorry we have to be leaving now, and it's been lovely meeting you again, Kate, love, but we have a train to catch.'

'It's been lovely meeting you two, too, after so many long years. But I was thinking you could come home with me and meet my family, and have a good old chat about those old days. Perhaps another time.'

'I don't know about that, Kate. We're planning to make our home in Australia as soon as we sell everything. But we will certainly get your books to read, and will come and visit you before we go, and write to yer.'

I felt rather sad having to say goodbye to them, and as I was writing my address for them I felt I would never see them again, but as they both promised to write, I hoped they wouldn't forget. As we walked outside the Jeweller's Arms I shook hands with them both, when Joe said, 'Do yer mind, Kate, if we both kiss yer?'

As I held up my face, they both hugged and kissed me full on my lips. Every passer-by stopped to smile and stare, but I didn't feel a bit embarrassed when they both gave me an extra big hug and squeeze.

'The last time we kissed you, Kate, was when we was trying to sell the smelly herring-boxes for a living.'

How well I recalled those sad times, many years ago!

As I waved them both goodbye, my tears began to flow. They were the first two people I had met on my walks, only now to lose them again so soon. Yet I hoped they would keep their promise and that one day soon I would hear from them both, or meet them again.

Today, I am still hoping, and waiting.

# My Mum

I never knew my mum's parents, yet often when she and Dad came back from the pub at night they'd sit talking by the fire. They didn't know I was in the room, so I used to hear snatches of conversation. One night I heard Mum talk about the workhouse where she was born and put into service when she was thirteen. Other times she'd say how cruel her mother had been. And I wondered if she was tainted the same, for when anyone was cruel people used to say, 'They can't help it, it's in their blood.' As a child, brought up in ignorance, this puzzled me somehow.

When I asked my brother Frankie, he said he didn't know either. Now my brother wasn't so nervous of Mum as I was, so he decided to ask her if we had any grandparents or uncles and aunts on her side. One night, as Dad and Mum came in from the pub, Frankie decided to do it then and there. As soon as they sat down, he piped up at once, 'Mum, where's our grandad an' gran'ma?'

'Why do yer wanta know that all of a sudden?' she cried.

'Well, all the other kids in the yard 'ave 'em, an' uncles an' aunts.'

Suddenly she got up out of the chair and slapped his face.

'Yo wanta know *too* much. Anyway, yo'll be none the wiser fer knowin'. Any'ow, they're in 'eaven, God rest their souls,' she added.

It would have been wiser if Frankie had left it at that, but he was sulking now. As soon as he saw Dad go upstairs, he cried, 'How do yer know they're in 'eaven, they might be in the other place stokin' up the fire fer yo.'

Suddenly Mum flew at my brother and gave him two more hard clouts across his face. 'That one's fer yer bloody cheek, an' the other's fer speakin' bad of the dead!'

Why our parents never talked to us about their parents we could never understand. When we asked any kind of question, we *should* have been told. It was always 'Yer know enough to goo on with', or 'Kids should be seen an' not 'eard.' But my brother and I, the first chances we got, we always cleared out of Mum's way, especially when things didn't go right. We had more fun and affection with our little school friends with whom we played in the side streets.

There's no climbing up a lamppost today.

Those iron posts were fun for us girls and boys, swinging a piece of rope over the iron arm that jutted out beneath the gas lamp. And if we couldn't manage to find a piece of rope, we would tie together plaited straw from empty orange-boxes and swing around backwards, forwards, backwards, forwards, ten times, then others in line took their turn. Or you would see the lads sitting on the edge of the pavement beneath the light from the street lamp, reading their swapped comics, or telling dirty stories, or skimming used tram tickets, to see who could skim the furthest.

Sometimes when our parents were out, the gas man would call to empty the pennies from the meter.

We would watch him tip the pennies on to the table and count them – sometimes there would be a penny or twopence over.

'Now give this to yer mum,' he'd say.

But this was *our* little treat – until we were found out.

I remember our gas meter was fastened to the wall, halfway down the cellar steps. I could never understand why our mum was the only one to put the pennies in the meter – other times she was too scared to go *near* the cellar. (Only by chance did I find out why.)

Some nights we would be sitting by the fire, when all at once we would see the gas light begin to flicker. Nobody would offer to go and put a penny in. But as soon as Jack, my eldest brother, came home, Mum would ask him if he could spare a penny, or sit in the dark.

'Wot, agen!' he'd cry. 'There must be summat wrong with that bloody meter. It must wait for me,' he added angrily.

'It only wants a penny in, Jack. I'll give it yer back later,' she replied.

'I've 'eard that befower! But it's funny ter me it wants feedin' wen I cum 'ome. Any'ow,' he added, 'I don't think yer gettin' enough gas for the pennies yer put in, yer betta see the gas man agen.'

'I will,' she replied. As she picked up the penny he'd slung on the table, she walked towards the cellar steps and dropped the penny in her black apron pocket. Mum knew Jack had been afraid to go down the cellar since he was bitten by a rat.

As soon as the gas flared up again she came into the room, all smiles.

Then one night, I happened to be alone in the house when all at once the light began to flicker. I knew soon I'd be in the dark and I was scared. Suddenly I thought of the rent money Mum always kept in the empty tea caddy on the mantelshelf. Quickly, I took a penny and went down to the cellar. But try as I could, I couldn't get that penny in the slot, until I heard several clicks and another penny that was already wedged in fell. I put the other penny in, then when I turned the knob again and heard it fall, I realised why Mum always went down to the meter. She'd put a penny in, turn it halfway, therefore she'd get only half the gas. Having pocketed Jack's penny, she'd finish the first penny already there.

I never told her how I found out. But that same night, as we sat round the fire, I was watching Mum looking up on the wall waiting for the gas to flicker, when all at once Jack said, 'Did yer tell the gas man about the meter, Mum?'

'No, I dain't. Why?' she replied, still glancing up at the gas mantle.

'Well, it's funny you don't ask me for a penny ternight.'

Suddenly I piped up, 'There's no need, Jack, *I've* put a penny in.'

Mum stared hard at me, daggers drawn, as she demanded, 'An' where did yer get yer penny from?'

'I was afraid to be in the dark, so I took a penny out of the tea caddy. But I couldn't get it in at first, because there was already one stuck in the slot.'

13

Mum never said another word, but next day she gave me a thrashing with the cane. When I asked what it was for, she said, 'That's fer tekin' a penny from the rent without askin'.' But I wasn't all that green. I knew the real reason.

# My Dad

During the whole of 1930 and even before, men talked of a war with Germany. Unemployed men who stood lounging on street corners were heard to say that if it did come they would be glad to join up, if only to get the King's shilling for a meal and a few fags. But little did they know that bad news was to come sooner than they expected. In fact, the streets and their lives would never be the same again, nor for millions of people throughout the world.

That dreaded morning came, as old men and young alike, who hadn't got the price of a pint of beer, crowded into the pub, the George and Dragon, to hear Churchill's voice over the wireless, announcing that we were at war with Germany.

'Hitler won't start on us, 'e's too scared,' old Joe Bishop cried out.

'Yer right theea, Joe me ole mate,' his friend piped up. 'The bleedin' Kaiser couldn't lick us, so wot chance 'as that bleedin' shot-up paper 'anger got?'

'But we gorra be prepared,' Billy Turner replied. 'Look what 'e's done ter Czechoslovakia, and Poland now 'e's got 'is bloody eyes on. Anyway, they ain't got nothin' ter stop 'im with, an' 'e knows it.'

'Neither 'ave we, Bill, unless our sleepy bloody government wakes up afower it's too late, an' if they don't do summat soon, we shall be in the same boat.'

'But dain't Hitler sign an agreement with old Neville Chamberlain?' Fred asked.

'Wot! A piece of paper! Wot good was that? An' now we're in it,' Billy replied.

As soon as Churchill had finished speaking, the boss of the George and Dragon, who had lost a leg in the first war, gave them all a free pint of beer.

'Drink up, me lads,' he cried out from behind the counter. 'The drinks are on the 'ouse.'

He was a jovial fellow, and as he and the barmaid pulled pint after pint, he told them, 'When yer join up, remember ter kill off a few German bastards fer me, an' yer can 'ave the loan of me wooden leg ter crack 'em with, in case yer run out of bullets. But don't forget ter bring it back,' he added.

Everybody laughed at the publican's humour. Yet little did they know that many would never see the George and Dragon again, or their cheerful landlord, for this was a war not only for men but for women and children too, and millions would lose their homes and loved ones.

I still recall those many years ago, when I was eleven, in 1914 when the First World War started. My brother Jack and my brother Charles couldn't wait for their call-up papers, like a good many lads who were unemployed. My dad too tried to enlist, but when he went to Thorp Street recruiting offices, he was told they wanted only younger men. Dad went wild. He told them he'd been a sergeant in the Boer War and knew more about the army than they would ever learn. But he did his bit to help in the war effort – he gave up chopping and selling firewood and went to work in Great Russell Street opposite St George's Church, where he worked in a casting shop making shell cases. I recall my dad had a scar about six inches long down the left side of his cheek. He never said how he got it, and we never asked. But I remember, one day, Mum telling the landlord one of the Boers gave it him, before he killed him.

I loved my dad. He was always kind and gentle, so different from my mother. I didn't grumble when she often made my brother Frankie and me take our dad's dinner to his works. When we left school at twelve o'clock, she would have a basin of stew already wrapped in a clean towel.

But Dad never let us see inside the yard where he worked, he always met us outside the wooden gates, and after taking from us the basin and the few coppers Mum supplied for his beer, he'd hand us yesterday's dirty empty basin to take back home.

'Now be off with yer or you'll be late for school,' he often used to say. But if we asked him if we could come inside the gates and watch him work, he would always reply that fumes from the sulphur would kill us.

But being two inquisitive kids, we decided that one day we would get in that yard and see for ourselves what he did.

That day came when we had a holiday, St George's Day. It was very warm, so off we went, Frankie and I, to explore. When we came to the big wooden gates, try as we might, they wouldn't budge. But as we walked away, disappointed, we spotted a horse and wagon loaded with sand. As soon as we saw the driver pull up outside those gates, we hid in St George's churchyard and waited. Soon we saw Dad open the gates wide, and in went the driver with the horse and his load. As we crept near the gates we noticed that Dad had left the driver to empty the cart. Now this was our chance. Quickly we crept into the yard and hid behind a big pile of brown sand and a mountain of coke. Soon the driver and the horse left, and as we looked around we saw that the yard was full of old wooden crates and broken riddles, and beneath the dirty iron-framed windows were three different kinds of sand – red, brown and white. And on the other side of the wall was burnt-out coke, still smouldering.

The smells were awful. I wanted to run away, but my brother pulled me back. 'No yer don't!' he managed to whisper. 'If Dad does catch us, we're in this together.' So I had to stay.

We had to wipe the dirt and sand off one of the small square panes of broken glass before we could see anything, and as we stood on a mountain of sand we managed to see inside: a long well-worn wooden bench, on one end an anvil, a large iron vice and several steel rasps. Everything was covered in sand, from the floor to the walls and ceiling. Brass castings and lumps of metal were strewn everywhere. We strained our necks to see further, but not until we noticed that a couple of the small windows were missing, so we could look through. The only other light was from a broken fanlight high up in the roof. As soon as we saw our dad at the other end of the room, we almost gave ourselves away as the smell of the fumes from the melting hot metal and sulphur wafted at us. But we still watched as he tied his muffler over his nose and mouth. He was clad only in his corduroy trousers; we saw his two large tattooed angels from the back of his neck to his waist sweating too, and as he bent over the hole in the ground, which was the furnace, we saw him grip a pair of long iron tongs and lift out what looked like a red-hot stone bucket. Beneath his feet was a wooden tray with patterns in sand, and as we watched him pour the boiling metal into the tray below, yellow, green and purple sulphur fumes wafted at us. We nearly choked. We slid down that mountain of sand and ran through the gates and into the street. We never went past those gates again. Although we still took Dad's dinner every day, he never knew we had seen him at work.

Often the doctor warned our dad about the sulphur fumes getting into his lungs. He still did his bit for his country and carried on until 1918. Then he was thrown on the scrapheap like thousands of other men as soon as the war ended, on the dole and the means test. A few years later my dad died in the Western Road Workhouse. When my daughter Jean was born, I often visited him. But sad to say, he lay in his bed, not recognising me. I often quarrelled with my mother and sisters and brothers for allowing him to die in such a horrible place.

# The Mouse Trap

My brother Frankie and I were always hungry and looked forward to going to school where each morning, before we started our lessons, we were given two slices of bread and jam and a mug of cocoa, which our parents could ill afford.

These were often supplied to all the poor children from the slum areas at St Paul's School in Camden Drive by our vicar, Canon Smith of St Paul's Church.

After leaving school at twelve o'clock, we would all rush home like little ants, hungry for our next feed, which might be scratching stew, or any other kind of food hashed up from leftovers from the days before.

My brother and I often begged for food outside the factory gates as people left. And each night before going to bed we had a piece of bread and dripping, while Mum and Dad sat down to bread and cheese and a Spanish onion.

Often our mouths would water at the very thought of it.

Dad also had his usual pint of beer, with a good head of froth on top. This was called 'The Long Pull', and in those days it cost twopence.

One night, while my mum and dad were out, my brother whispered, 'Katie, I'd luv some of that cheese.'

'An' me,' I replied. 'But Mum alwis locks it away in the chiffonier.'

'Ah, but I know 'ow ter get at it,' he replied, winking at me.

'But 'ow can yer? She keeps the key down inside 'er blouse.'

'I don't need the key, yer simply pull out the top drawer an' put yer 'and down inside an' lift the cheese out.'

'No, Frankie!' I cried. 'Mum's sure ter find out, an' if she does she'll kill us both.'

'If 'er does find out, I'll tek the blame, Katie, an' say it was me, but you'll 'ave ter put yower 'and down inside 'cause yer 'and's smaller than mine.'

I didn't feel so nervous when he said he'd take the blame.

But we didn't have the chance. Mum came back early that night. The following night, as soon as Mum and Dad were ready to go out, Mum told us to hurry ourselves and eat our bread and dripping and get off to bed. 'An' mind yer don't drop any of them crumbs on the flowa, we've got enough mice runnin' around the rooms.'

As soon as they left the house, we knew they wouldn't be back till after the George and Dragon closed at eleven o'clock. I stood and watched my brother pull out the top drawer. As he placed it on the table, he told me to feel down inside, where I'd find the chunk of cheese. After putting my hand down on to the ledge below, I just managed to lift the cheese out. As I placed it on the table, trembling all over in case Mum and Dad came home early, Frankie sorted in the drawer for a sharp knife, then carefully cut us each a thin sliver, and after I had put the rest of the cheese back, he pushed the drawer in.

This went on for three nights. Mum never said anything, so we felt safe.

Then one night, as we sat eating our meagre supper, we saw Mum unlock the chiffonier door, and as soon as she put the cheese on the table she yelled, 'Sam! You'll 'avta get me another mouse trap!'

'Yo've already got fower, wot yer want another one for?'

'Well, look at this piece of cheese! It seems ter be gooin' down very quick.'

'All right, all right,' replied Dad impatiently. 'I'll bring yer one from me work. Now let's 'ave no mower shoutin'! An' get me me supper, I'm clammed.'

While Mum was cutting the cheese and onion, I could feel her eyes on us both. Later, when I whispered to Frankie that I thought Mum knew it was us, he replied, 'Don't be daft, she still thinks the mice 'ave bin at it, any'ow she would 'ave said.'

We didn't try again until that piece of cheese had been used up. The following weekend Mum bought a larger piece, so we decided to try our luck again. But at the last moment I got scared: 'We betta not, Frankie. I've still a feelin' she knows it's us, the way she looks at us.'

''Ow can she, when she's got the key? Cum on, don't be scared, tell yer wot, we'll just 'ave a nibble around the edges an' when she sees teeth marks, she'll think the mice 'ave cum back agen.'

So out came the top drawer again and out came the cheese. I began to nibble one side and Frankie nibbled the other. But when he held the cheese and gazed at it longingly, I heard him say, 'It would be worth a beltin' from Dad to 'ave a good bite at it.'

'No, Frankie! No! Put it back, please,' I cried.

'OK. It was just a thought,' he replied, grinning at me.

Quickly I snatched the cheese from him and put it back where I'd found it. As soon as the drawer was pushed in, we went up to bed. That night I lay awake thinking he might go back downstairs and risk a thrashing by eating a lump. After hearing him get out of bed to use our makeshift bucket for a wee, I couldn't settle until I felt him crawl back to his place at the foot of the bed.

The following night we tried again, but as I felt around the ledge I began to scream – my finger was caught in a mouse trap. I pulled my hand out and ran around the room, screaming for all I was worth, with the mouse trap hanging from my finger.

'Frankie! Frankie!' I kept screaming. 'Pull it off! Pull it off!'

As soon as he released the spring I saw blood on the trap where my finger had been. After he had found a piece of rag and wrapped it, I began to weep.

'She'll know for sure now it's us, when she sees the trap,' I sobbed as my tears fell.

'Don't cry, Katie, I'll put it back an' if 'er does find out, I'll tek the blame, but try an' 'ide yer finger, an' if she does ask don't say nothink. I know wot ter say.'

Then came that Friday night, which was our bread, brimstone and black treacle night. (This was what Mum called our physic.) As we sat at the table, I tried my best to hide my finger beneath my pinafore. As soon as Mum began to open the chiffonier door, I began to tremble all over. Then I saw her throw the cheese and the trap across the table.

'Them bloody mice 'ave bin at it agen, Sam!' she yelled.

'Ain't yer caught them, then?'

'No! But wotever it was must 'ave bin caught, 'cause theeas the trap with the blood on it.'

Dad picked up his newspaper to begin reading. I wished the floor would open up and I could vanish as I saw Mum notice my finger.

'Wot yer bin up ter?' she cried.

Before I could open my mouth, Frankie said, 'It was an accident.'

'Wot yer mean, an accident?' she demanded.

'I 'it it with the 'ammer.'

Suddenly Dad glared at him over the top of his paper. 'Wot did yer say?'

'Katie was 'oldin' me fire can an' while I was knockin' a nail in the 'ammer slipped.'

'I'll knock a bloody nail in yow, me lad, if I see yer with another fire can – now get yer grub down yer! An' get up them stairs, the pair of yer!'

We didn't need telling twice.

Next day my finger began to throb and was very painful. I was too scared to tell my mum, or even show it to her, but I had to show it to someone. The only person was Mrs Taylor, our kind neighbour. I knocked on the door, and as she opened it and glanced down at that piece of filthy rag round my finger I began to weep.

'Wot's the matter, luv? Wot yer done? Yer betta cum in an' tell me.'

As she sat me down on an orange-box I cried, 'I've done a terrible thing, Mrs Taylor, an' I'm afraid me mum and dad's gooin' ter find out an' me finger's painin' me summat awful.'

'Now wipe yer eyes an' tell me all about it.'

When I told her she cried, 'Yer wicked, wicked wench! Ye'll both be punished as sure as God made little apples! Now stop yer blartin' an' let me get that filthy rag off an' see wot yo've done.'

I began to scream with pain as she tried to snatch the rag off, but the blood had dried up and it was stuck. I was ready to run out, but she held me firm, and when I'd calmed down she got some hot water and salt and after bathing the rag came off. As soon as she saw my finger all bruised and bent she suddenly exclaimed as she crossed herself, 'Mary Mother of God, the end of yer finger's broke!'

'Can yer mend it, Mrs Taylor? It's 'urtin' summat awful.'

'There ain't nothink I can do fer that! Yo'll afta go ter the 'orspital an' get it seen to.'

'Can yer cum with me, Mrs Taylor?' I pleaded. 'I'm afraid of 'orspitals an' doctors.'

'I can't, luv, I've gotta get me washin' finished ready for the pawnshop, but I'll get our Minnie ter tek yer.'

'If I goo, yer won't tell me mum what I've told yer or she'll kill me.'

'Yer poor wench, I understand. I won't say a word, now sit theea while I put a piece of clean rag on, then afta yer drink this 'ot cuppa tea I'll call me niece.'

I thanked her and waited while she went to call her niece. Minnie Taylor was twelve, two years older than me. I never had much to do with her because she was always swearing and telling lies. But I was glad she was coming with me, for I knew I was too scared to face a doctor on my own. Her aunt explained that I'd broken my finger, and I was pleased she hadn't told her how.

'Cum on, Katie, I'll tek yer, I ain't afraid of bloody doctors nor 'orspitals,' she cried as soon as her aunt was out of hearing.

We hurried up Spring Hill towards Dudley Road Hospital and came to the rusty wrought-iron gates. Minnie tried to push them open, but they were locked. Even the gates scared me. I was about to change my mind and turn back when I felt Minnie catch hold of my frock. Suddenly she pulled me towards the gates, just as a very tall elderly man dressed in a long white gown, looking very stern and forbidding, came down the path. As he made his way towards the gates he bawled out, 'Wot yo two kids want?'

I was too scared to answer, but I knew Minnie was scared of no one. She shouted through the bars, 'It's me friend 'ere, Katie. I've brought 'er ter see yer, Doctor.'

'I ain't a doctor! I'm the lodge-keeper. An' yer can't cum in 'ere!' he snapped.

'But we've cum a lung way, so yer betta open these gates an' let us in, 'cause me friend 'as broke 'er finger and the doctor's gotta mend it.'

'Yer can't cum in 'ere unless yer mother brings yer.'

'But I ain't got a muvver,' she replied.

'Well, tell yer friend ter tell *er* mother ter cum.'

'She ain't got a muvver either,' she lied. 'So yo'll 'ave ter let us in.'

'Not until an adult cums with yer.'

'Adult? Adult? Wot's them?' shouted Minnie.

'Yo'll soon find out when I open these gates an' clout yer bleedin' 'ear'oles, now bugger orf the pair of yer!'

As soon as I saw him start fumbling for his keys, I was ready to run, but Minnie stayed to give him a bit more cheek. 'Bugger orf yerself, yer miserable old bleeda!' she yelled as she stopped to put her tongue out at him. We saw him put the key into the lock. We ran as fast as we could.

As soon as we got as far as Icknield Street we stopped to get our breath, and I managed to say, 'Minnie, yer shouldn't 'ave told 'im we ain't got a muvver. Wot if 'e finds out?'

'I don't care, but I 'ad ter tell 'im summat 'opin' 'e'd let us in.'

When Minnie told her aunt what had happened, she gave her a piece of bread pudding and told her that her mother was waiting for her. As soon as Minnie had closed the door behind her, Mrs Taylor said, 'Never mind Katie, luv, it'll 'eal up in time an' if you'll cum in every day after yer leave school I'll bathe and dress it for yer.'

After I had thanked her, I left to go home. As soon as

Frankie saw me he asked how my finger was. I told him it seemed a bit better now Mrs Taylor had treated it. Suddenly he yelled, 'Yer dain't tell 'er wot 'appened, did yer?'

'Yes, Frankie, I 'ad to,' I replied, as tears ran down my cheeks.

'Now it'll be all over the street, an' Mum an' Dad will 'ear about it.'

'Nobody will know, she's promised not to tell anyone,' I whimpered.

I was glad I hadn't told him about Minnie and the hospital.

'Well, if they do find out I'll say it was only me, now wipe yer tears and let's go ter the rec and play Tip Cat.'

That following Monday morning while I was at school my teacher noticed the rag on my finger. When she asked what I'd done I replied, 'I think I've broke me finger, Miss.'

'Well, you'd better have a note and have it treated at the clinic,' she replied impatiently.

That afternoon I went reluctantly to the school clinic in Great Charles Street. This was where children went with all sorts of complaints, even to have their heads shaved for lice. But when I got to the door and saw a woman coming out holding a bloody rag to a little boy's mouth, my courage failed me. I turned back, and as I came down Great Hampton Street I called at Snape's the chemist's. With the few pennies I'd got hidden down my stocking I went up to the counter and asked for a finger bandage and some lint. While Mr Snape turned his back to reach down a box, I quickly pulled up the three pennies. 'That'll be fourpence,' he said.

'But I only got threepence, can I bring yer the other penny next week?'

'Sorry, me dear, I'll 'ave ter cut the lint in half,' he replied.

As soon as I got home I hid the lint and bandage until I was alone. Each night I bathed my finger in salt water, then wrapped it.

My teacher, glad to say, never questioned me when she saw my finger wrapped in a clean bandage.

\* \* \*

As I grew older I was no longer scared of my mum. I remember the day I was eighteen – I thought now was the best time to tell her how Frankie and I stole the cheese. Imagine my surprise when she said, 'I knew it was yow two.'

'Yer knew? All them many years ago? An' yer never said a word?'

'No! Because I set the trap fer yer, an' thought you'd bin punished enough. Now you've got the end of yer finger broke ter prove it.'

Ever since I can remember my mother and I were never very close, but after she told me about that night I wondered how cruel she could be.

Often, when I'm trimming that fingernail, I remember how that mouse trap clung to it.

# My Grandma

My Grandma Hannah was an eccentric, lonely old woman, poor but very proud. She lived in a tumbledown old house like ours. Although she was well known in and around the district, she would never have anything to do with the neighbours. She hated gossiping tongues.

Often she could be seen and heard smacking her lips as she sucked a lozenge drop, or a pear drop, on her toothless gums. She knew, too, how many were in a two-ounce paper cone. When she sent me to the little sweet shop she always counted them, and gave me one.

'That's for bein' honest,' she would say.

Once or twice a week, she would be seen in her well-worn old Salvation Army uniform and bonnet, shuffling towards our local mission hall. Other times she would be wearing her old black alpaca frock – which had seen better days and always swept the pavement – with a black bonnet and knitted shawl. On her feet she wore elastic-sided boots.

Apart from her uniform, I never saw her wear anything but black, and she always carried a strong crooked stick. Many of the kids from my school often called her an old witch, but if she happened to hear them she'd curse and threaten them with the stick. God knows what she would have done if she had caught one of them, for she feared no one.

Whenever I saw or heard any of the kids shout after her, I would await my opportunity and as soon as I saw my chance I would fight like an alley cat. But sometimes I got the worst of these battles, for I had my mum to contend with as well.

But she was my granny and I loved her. Many times when my mum wanted me out of the way I used to go to Granny's and run her errands and do little jobs, like fetching a quarter of a hundredweight of coal in a trolley, or going to the butcher's for three pennyworth of bits (scrag ends), or to the grocer's for two pennyworth of bacon bones.

'An' tell 'im not ter shave all the bacon off the bones,' she used to say.

She was stubborn, too, and very seldom paid her rent. One day I happened to be there when the rent man knocked on the door, and as she made her way towards the stairs she whispered, 'Tell 'im ter call next wick an' I'll 'ave summat for 'im then.'

I don't know whether he saw her through a wide crack in the door, but as I gave the message he called out, 'And see that yer do, or it's the last chance!'

But Granny was not on her own – several neighbours got into arrears too. The rent in those days, during and before the 1914 war, was only 3s. 6d. a week, and if they couldn't pay something off the arrears, many had the bailiffs. Often I'd seen people bolt their doors on the inside and lie quiet until they passed. But at the first chance, the bailiffs would take off the door and carry it away.

I remember one bitterly cold foggy night, our door was taken away and my dad nailed up a piece of sacking, and when my brother Jack came home on leave he mistook it for the door and fell head first into the room, kit bag and all.

Later, Mum managed to make a bundle for the pawnshop, and with a loan from my married sister the door was soon back on again. But some were luckier than others – they did a moonlight flit. It often used to surprise me that my granny never lost her door; she was even more stubborn than my mum.

Whenever any bills were pushed under her door, she would tear them up and throw them in the dustbin. Other bills she would roll together and lay in the fender ready to put under the wood sticks to light the fire, and if some were soft paper she would fold them away, for her bum paper. She never wasted anything.

Sometimes on my school holidays I'd go and run her errands and sweep and dust the old well-worn furniture, which she didn't have much of. Often, I would see a mouse scurry down a hole in the wainscot. But I was never afraid of them, neither was my granny, for I was used to seeing both mice and rats, and many times I got into trouble when I put a few crumbs down by the hole.

One Friday afternoon I came home from school with a rash on my face and arms. I couldn't stop my nose running, and I was feeling sick. No one was at home, so I made my way to my granny's house. As soon as she saw me she cried, 'Wipe your snotty nose!' I wiped it with a piece of rag she pushed towards me. But when she took a second look she asked, ''Ow long 'ave yer 'ad that rash on yer face?'

'Since yesterday, Granny,' I replied.

''As yer mum seen it?'

'Yes, she said it's a cold I've got.'

'Don't look like a cold ter me!' she answered. 'Anyway,' she added, 'yer betta come over by the winda where I can see yer betta.'

As I stood in the light, she told me, 'Pull yer frock up an' tek yer drawers down, while I 'ave a good look at yer.' After inspecting my bum, and then my back, she turned me round to inspect my belly. Suddenly she tut-tutted and announced, 'I thought as much! You've got German measles,' and as I began to cry she said, 'You can't goo back 'ome now in this cold night air, yer betta stay 'ere in the warm where I can keep me eye on yer.'

'But Mum will be wonderin' where I am,' I replied.

'If I know anythink about yer mum, she won't care, as lung as she knows I'm lookin' after yer. Now cum on, wipe yer nose, yer stayin' 'ere!'

I'd never stayed at my granny's for more than a couple of hours when I helped her and ran her errands, so I looked forward to staying. She made me a makeshift bed on an old horsehair sofa she kept in her bedroom.

After lighting the fire in the old iron grate, she gave me a cup of watered-down warm milk, covered me over with an old grey blanket, and as she tucked it round me she said, 'Now yo'll be all right. I shan't be lung, I'm gooin' ter the

29

chemist an' get yer some saffron tea, then I'll call an' tell yer mum where yo are.'

That small bedroom became very warm; I quickly fell asleep, but soon I was awakened by my mum prodding me.

'Cum on! I knew I'd find yer 'ere! An' wot's them spots on yer face?' she added.

'Granny says I got German measles,' I managed to say as tears fell.

'Well, yer betta get dressed an' cum 'ome, an' I'll get the doctor.'

Just then, Granny walked in.

'Yo'll leave 'er where 'er is, Polly! Yer wanta kill the child? Yo ain't tekin' 'er out of 'ere in this cold night air!'

'Very well,' I heard Mum reply as she went down the stairs, 'but if anythink 'appens to 'er I won't be responsible. Yer know yer spoilin' 'er,' she added.

'She'll be betta looked after in my care than in yowen!' I heard Granny reply before the door slammed.

During the day, Granny put a paper blind up to the window to keep the light from my eyes, and that half-light I had to contend with until I was better, except at night when she lit a piece of candle. Ever since I can remember I was always a nervous child with a very vivid imagination and, being undernourished, I wept at the least thing.

As I began to feel better and saw the rash was disappearing, I told her I wanted to go home and back to school.

Suddenly she stared hard at me. 'Yo ain't fit enough yet!' she snapped. 'Any'ow, we'll see wot the docta ses when 'e comes!'

I could see she was angry as she added, 'Ain't I looked afta yer betta than yer mum?'

'Yes, Granny, but I'm missing my schooling,' I replied as the tears began to fall.

'Now, I don't want any blartin'! If you'll promise to lie quiet I'll tell yer some funny stories.'

I loved her when she didn't lose her temper with me, but she had changeable moods, like Mum.

Often when she sat on her bed facing me, telling me fairy

stories, I would fall asleep. One night I asked her if she remembered her mum, when she was a little girl.

She replied, 'It's a lung story, Katie luv; when yer older I'll tell yer.'

'But didn't you ever go ter school?' I asked, for I knew she couldn't read or write.

'No,' she replied. 'I 'ad ter goo into service. Now goo ter sleep.'

But one night she did tell me that her mother used to hide her away in the attic when she heard the Mormons were about.

When I asked her to explain why, she said, 'They carried little girls away and took 'em ter Salt Lake City.'

I was just about to ask more questions when she shuffled her way down the stairs to make my nightly cocoa.

She seemed to be such a long time coming back that I wondered if she'd gone out and left me alone – everything seemed so quiet, and I was scared as I watched the flickering light of the candle making ghostly shadows on the bare whitewashed walls. My imagination got the better of me. Just as that small piece of candle burnt itself out, I began to scream.

As soon as Granny came into the room, she yelled, 'Now wot's the matter with yer?'

'The candle's gone out an' I thought you'd left me,' I whimpered. When she had lit another piece, she glared down at me.

''Ere's yer cocoa!' she cried as she slopped the cup down on the chair beside the sofa. 'Now,' she added, 'I want no mower silly screamin'! An' don't be such a big babby!'

As soon as I had finished drinking the cocoa she took the lighted candle, and as she shuffled her way towards the stairs I became scared of the dark again, but when I asked her to leave the candle she grew angrier.

'I ain't leavin' no light!' she shouted. 'Yo've slept in the dark befower, now get ter sleep!'

'But I'm frightened of the dark now, Granny, please leave the candle,' I pleaded.

31

'No, and I mean no!' she yelled over her shoulder. 'An' if yer don't lie down now, the bogey man will come an' get yer!'

That was the worst thing she could have yelled at me. When I heard her footsteps on the stairs, I covered my head with the old grey blanket and cried myself to sleep.

As soon as I was well again, I went back home and the next day I started back to school. But I never forgot my granny's warning – it was still there in the back of my mind. I wasn't afraid when I was back home, where I slept with my sister and brother. Nevertheless, I was still afraid to be out in the street when it was dark.

One afternoon, my mum sent me to the corner shop for two pennyworth of jam in a cup.

'An' 'urry yerself afower it gets dark,' I remember her saying.

I crossed the horse-road and entered the shop. Several women were waiting to be served. I knew that by the time it was my turn it would be dark. Boldly I walked up to the counter and asked Mr Baker to serve me.

'Yo wait yer turn! Any'ow, wot yer want?' he cried out for all to hear.

'Me mum wants two pennorth of jam,' I replied as I handed him the cup.

'Well, yer can goo back an' tell yer mum I don't run me shop on 'er two pennorths.'

Just as I was about to leave, one kind woman said I could take her turn. Although the others at the back began to sniff and grumble, the woman ignored them. But there were still two women to be served before me. As soon as it was my turn, Mr Baker stopped to light the gas jet on the wall. I knew now it must be getting dark outside. I began to get nervous. He took my cup and weighed it, then spooned the jam in from a large crock jar. As he took the twopence he cried, "Ere's yer jam! An' tell yer mother this is the last two pennorth she'll get from 'ere until she pays some off the strap book!'

'Skinny old skinflint!' I thought. If only I'd been older, I would have told him where he could stick his jam.

When I got into the street it was nearly dark, so I began to hurry. Just as I turned the corner, I had the fright of my life as I came face to face with a black man. Suddenly, I thought this was the bogey man my granny had warned me about, for I'd never seen a black man before. I screamed, dropped the cup and ran for my life.

As I fell indoors, Mum wanted to know what was wrong.

'Mum, Mum, Mum,' I kept repeating. 'I've just seen the bogey man!'

'Wot yer mean, yer seen a bogey man?' she exclaimed.

'I *did*, an' 'e was black all over, an' 'e grinned at me!'

I could see she didn't believe me.

'But where's the jam I sent yer for?'

'I dropped it in the horse-road, and ran,' I replied, beginning to weep.

She still wouldn't believe me, until she took me back to the shop. But when we got there, we both saw the remains of the broken cup and two mongrel dogs licking the jam.

I was put to bed that night with a caning, and no piece of bread and jam.

That was the first black man I'd ever seen.

After school hours I still visited my granny and ran her errands, but I *never* stayed until it was dark. Although she was a funny old gran – she made me both laugh and cry – I loved her at times. But when I was about ten years old she died. Often I wept, thinking only of the kindness and understanding she *tried* to give me.

I still think of her today and tell my great-grandchildren about her, and of some of the stories she used to tell me.

# Scriptures and Safety Pins

Our living-room, like many rooms in our district, was not even large enough to swing a cat. So in very warm weather my mum, like the rest of the neighbours, would bring out one of the old backless wooden chairs, and peel and scrape potatoes into the tin bowl. These potatoes were a luxury for Sunday dinner. Other days we had fried leftovers. Some Sundays she would make believe she had a joint of meat to carve. She would bring out the carving knife and sing at the top of her voice for all the neighbours to come out and see her sharpening the knife on the window-ledge. Over the years that sandstone window-ledge, as well as the step, looked more and more like a half moon.

Mum would buy the cheapest and smallest potatoes she could find. She always said they stretched further, but many were too small even to scrape. They were tipped into a bucket of water, where I had the job of swishing them around with a broken brick until the skin came partly off, and whatever didn't come off they were put in the pot to cook. Also in warm weather, Mum would sit outside on the step shelling the peas. Once, and only once, did I sit on that step beside her, but when she caught me pushing a few peas into my mouth she knocked me flying.

Another time, she said I could have a few empty shells. Others she saved to put on the back of the fire. Nothing was ever wasted in our house. Those pods tasted delicious after you took the outer skin off, and some I saved.

Getting a piece of string and making a line tied from the lamppost to the tap, I hung each pea shell. Then I'd call out, several times, 'Pin a pick, pin a pick, one pod for a pin, and two for a safety pin.' Kids would find pins from somewhere and pick the ones they fancied.

Another time I would cut pictures from newspapers. I had a craze for saving pins, hairpins too, but I found that other kids had the same idea. So *that* didn't go down too well – until one day I stood on the orange-box from the corner of the attic and climbed into the loft, where I found lots of odds and ends. But there was nothing of any use, until I spotted a large old book covered in dust. When I blew the dust off, I saw it was a Bible. As I mooched around on my hands and knees, I came across a coloured picture book. This too was thick with dust. I knew my mum always threw unwanted rubbish in the loft, yet I couldn't ever remember seeing these before. I hid them under my bed. The first opportunity I had to be alone, I cut out all the coloured pictures and placed each one inside the pages of the Bible. I didn't have enough to fill each page.

Next day was Saturday, and while Mum and Dad were shopping in the Bull Ring, I took the old backless wooden chair outside. As soon as I was sitting down with the heavy Bible on my lap I began to cry out, 'Pin a pick . . . come and pick yer own coloured picture. Two for a safety pin.'

Soon there were several kids with their pins trying their luck – one brought a hairpin and another even brought me a hatpin.

Those who drew a blank were unlucky, but I'd let them have two tries. If they failed again, I would show them which page to stick the pin in to save any squabbles. That day I was doing a roaring trade. I had quite a large cocoa tin full – until little Rosie Pumfry, who lived opposite, came running towards me holding two safety pins up in the air. She was about eight, three years younger than me, very small but very podgy, with little red fat cheeks and corn-coloured hair. She was an only child.

As soon as I took the pins and showed her where the pictures lay, she ran down the yard as if someone would stop and take them from her. She had been gone only a few minutes when I saw her mum dragging young Rosie towards me. She was trying to stop her ragged drawers from falling down. I guessed then where the two safety pins had come from. As she came near me she yelled, 'Now, you can just give me back them safety pins befower I clout yer bleedin' ear'ole.' I was often scared of this hard-faced little woman, but I found enough courage to say, 'Well, Mrs Pumfry, yer can 'ave yer pins back if yer give me me pictures back.'

'I put 'em on the fire, an' I ain't gooin' from 'ere till I get my pins,' she yelled.

I was really scared now, and I knew that all the kids were gathing around to see what was going to happen. But someone must have run to tell my mum. As soon as she came and saw the commotion, and heard what was going on, she called all the kids together, then tipped the full tin of pins on the floor. I began to cry when she told them to help themselves. Suddenly there was a free-for-all as the pins began to vanish. Then, as my mum handed two safety pins to Mrs Pumfry, I saw her drag little Rosie home, with her dirty drawers falling about her ankles as she wept.

Some of the kids laughed and pulled faces as Mum snatched up the Bible and dragged me indoors. As soon as she had slammed the door she threw the Bible on the table, then flung me across the room. 'Werd yer gettit?' she yelled.

'I found it in the loft, Mum,' I managed to answer.

'You tellin' the truth?' she replied, glaring at me.

'Yes, Mum.'

'Whose is it, do yer know?'

'No, Mum, I don't know whose it is.'

'Um, could be yer granny's, 'er was always 'idin' things away from me, but if it is, she's gooin' ter haunt yer for stickin' pins in that Bible.'

Suddenly I shouted loudly, 'But I dain't stick pins in it!'

'Don't yer dare raise yer bloody voice ter me, yer cheeky little varmint!' she yelled as she slapped my face. 'An' now, yer can get that chair in what yo've left outside, an' yer can tell them pin-pinchers what's listenin' outside me dower if they don't clear off, I'll be cummin' out an' chuck a bucket of water over 'em, an' it won't be only dirty water I'll be chuckin', either!'

They must have heard the warning. As soon as I opened the door they fled.

As I pushed that old wooden chair under the table, she began to bawl again: 'Now! Yer can goo an' put that Bible back where yer said yer found it, till I'm ready ter call yer down! An' yer can stop yer blartin'.'

As I turned to go up the stairs, she caught me putting my tongue out. She was ready to hit me again, but I was too quick. Before her hand came down, I snatched the Bible and fled up the stairs before she could grab me. But I knew I'd get my punishment later, even if it was several days later – she never forgot.

After I had put the Bible back in the loft, I lay down on the flock mattress and cried myself to sleep. I didn't even feel my sister Liza get in beside me. But when morning came and we were on our way to school, Liza asked me why I'd been crying in my sleep. When I told her what had happened she said, 'I knew it was Gran's Bible, she told me to 'ide it away before she died.'

'But why did she want to 'ide it away?' I asked.

''Cause me mum always 'ated seein' anythink of me gran's lyin' about.'

'But why would Mum wanta get rid of it?'

'Yer don't know our mum, Katie. But yer gotta lot ter learn yet afower yer much older.'

How true! I remembered those words in the years ahead.

# Rosie

Mrs Pumfry was a small woman in her mid-forties. Her greying hair was always pulled tightly over her ears and set in a bun in the nape of her neck. Her small dark eyes seemed always to stare out from her angular features and her thin lips drooped down at the corners, which made her look discontented and older than her years.

Whenever I happened to see her out in the yard, I would run back into the house and hide, for I was afraid of her since taking the two precious safety pins from Rosie.

But I hid once too often. When Mum asked me what was wrong I told her why I was afraid and what Mrs Pumfry might do to me.

'No need ter be afraid of 'er!' she exclaimed. ''Er bark's worse than 'er bite, so the best thing yer can do is ter knock on the dower an' say 'ow sorry yer are.'

As I stood wondering whether to go or not, Mum yelled as she pushed me outside, 'Goo on! An' do as yer told!'

When I knocked on the door, there was no answer. I was relieved in one way, but I knew that I had to get my message over. Quickly I knocked again – still no answer – but as I walked away I looked across the yard and saw Mrs Pumfry in the brewhouse, standing over the copper stirring the clothes over with the wooden boiler stick. As soon as she put the stick down in the sink she turned round, and as she wiped the hot steam from her face I blurted out quickly, 'Mrs Pumfry, I'm sorry I took those two safety pins off Rosie, but I didn't know they 'eld 'er drawers up.'

'No 'arm done, love,' she replied. 'But if you would like to 'elp me with the wringer . . .'

I knew now I was forgiven. I also helped her to peg the washing out on the line across the yard.

Mum never asked if I'd given her the message, but later I told her that Mrs Pumfry said I could call for Rosie any time. But whenever I did call, I could never understand why her mother always made me wait outside. Never once did she ask me in, nor any of her neighbours. They used to say she was stuck up because she owned a piano, yet no one ever heard it played. (People were lucky if they owned an old gramophone.) Plenty of gossip went around – people would say she wasn't married, a spinster left on the shelf with Rosie. But whatever she was she always ignored everyone, whether she heard them or not.

She went to church on Sunday mornings and evenings and sometimes of an afternoon to prayer meetings, and during these times Rosie was left alone to play with us children in the yard. This gave scope for more gossip. Talk went on – she must be meeting a 'fancy man'. Although there were plenty of Peeping Toms looking through their curtains, no one ever saw her bring anyone to the house.

One chilly afternoon I saw Rosie sitting on the doorstep crying. When I asked her why, she replied, 'I forgot to say me prayers last night an' me mum punished me.'

'Never mind, you go inside an' get warm, an' if yer want me to I'll come in an' stay with yer till yer mum comes 'ome.'

She stood up, nodded and wiped her eyes on her sleeve. I took hold of her hand and as we stepped inside, I realised that in all the three years they had lived there this was the first time I had entered her home. At once I noticed it was almost dark inside. The gas was going out.

'Do yer 'ave a penny for the meter?' I asked.

'Yes,' she replied. 'Me mum always leaves one on the shelf.'

After putting the penny in the meter, we came up the cellar steps into the living-room. I was surprised to see what a nice tidy room it was – not like our room, all cluttered up with everything in the wrong place. I noticed too that everything was old and well worn, but clean and highly polished. But what caught my eye most was the old piano against the wall facing the door. It had a roll-top lid, and two iron candle brackets jutting out from each side of the wooden music frame, and on the back of these was fretwork with faded red satin showing through. Also two rusty pedals. But for all that, I wished that I owned it. There was a piano stool beneath with an embroidered top, also faded and old.

'Does your mum play it?' I asked as I stared at it.

'No,' Rosie replied. 'She only opens it to dust and polish it.'

'Don't you play it neither?'

'No, I don't know 'ow to, any'ow Mum won't let me, even if I wanted to. She always keeps it locked.'

'But why does she keep it if it's never played?'

'She says she wouldn't part with it because it belonged to me Granny Pumfry. 'Ave you gotta piano?'

'No, we've only got an old gramophone with a brass trumpet. But that belongs to me brother Jack. 'E won't let us play it neither. But more often than not it's in the pawnshop, and Jack always carries the needles with him, and the sound-box. One day while he was out he forgot to take the soundbox. I looked everywhere for a needle, even a used one, but he must have put those away too. I was alone in the house, so I decided to get the chopper and chop a darning needle in two. With a bit of a struggle, Rosie, the needle snapped in two, so I put one half up the soundbox. I placed the soundbox on the record and as I turned the 'andle it gave a couple of moans and then the needle snapped and the soundbox fell on my brother's favourite record and cracked it. Me mum must 'ave been upstairs. Suddenly she came flying down. There was no time for me to run, so I got a walloping, and another when my brother Jack saw his favourite record in three pieces. After that, he always carried the handle and the soundbox with him, even if he was only going to the closet, to work, or out late at night, tomcatting.'

At that we both began to see the funny side and laughed together.

'But me and the rest of the kids in the street have lots of laughs when we put tissue paper over a comb and hold it to our lips and hum a tune. Sometimes we can't stop laughing when it tickles. We call it a jew's-harp,' I added.

The real jew's-harp is five thin bits of wire stretched across a small piece of plywood which cost threepence, which we couldn't afford, so that was our next best thing.

I left before Rosie's mum came home, but Rosie promised me she would try and find the key, then she would open the piano up and I could play.

One afternoon I was teaching her to play hopscotch, when all at once she stopped in the middle of the game and told me where her mother had hidden the piano key.

'Would yer like ter come and play a tune on it?' she asked.

'I'd love to, but what if yer mum comes 'ome and catches us?'

'She won't be back till five o'clock,' replied Rosie.

When we entered there was a bright fire glowing in the well black-leaded iron grate, and the kettle was already singing on the hob.

As soon as Rosie turned the key in the lock the piano lid rolled back with a few squeaks. But I was disappointed to see not black and white ivory keys but instead, staring at me, old and broken keys yellowed with age, like an old man's discoloured teeth – some missing too. But so as not to be too disappointed, I tried my one-finger exercise, 'God Save the King'. It was then that I realised also that some of the keys were dead, but after trying further up the scale I managed to finish part of the tune. When Rosie asked if I could play something else, I said I'd never had the chance. 'But I could if I 'ad plenty of practice,' I added.

'Well, if you'll come an' stay with me when me mum goes out you'd be able ter come an' practise.'

I'd always wanted to play a piano ever since my mum parted with the harmonium, but as this was now the only thing I could practise on I felt delighted. Each time the opportunity arose, I would go and play it while Rosie stood by to watch.

It wasn't long before I could play our national anthem with both hands.

Rosie and I were delighted, although it sounded out of key at times. Oh, if only some of the notes weren't missing – I'm sure it would have sounded better. Rosie made sure to lock it up and put the key back where she had found it, until the next time.

One Saturday afternoon I was very surprised when Rosie's mum knocked on our door and asked to see my mum. I was scared. Had she found out about me going into her house and opening up the piano? Guiltily I tried to hide, but it was too late. Mum had already called her in.

'Mrs Greenhill,' I heard her say, 'I was wondering if you could keep an eye on my Rosie for me. You see I 'ave to go to my brother's funeral today and I won't be back till about six o'clock.'

'Anything to oblige. Any'ow, Katie's 'ere, she'll keep 'er eye on 'er as well.'

After she'd gone, Mum said, 'Blimey, that's one out of the book. Fancy 'er comin' ter ask me. Anyway, Katie, you can both 'elp me in the brew'ouse an' after that I don't see why yer can't both go to number fifteen and wait until 'er mum comes 'ome. An' then yer can tell me all about what 'er's got, an' that piana the kids are talkin' about.'

After we had helped Mum we left to go out to play, and Rosie suggested I should go and have more practice. There was still a good two hours before Mrs Pumfry was due home, so we had plenty of time. But when we got indoors Rosie couldn't find the key anywhere. We tried prising the lid open with a knife, but when the knife snapped that was the end of that. Suddenly I thought about the bunch of keys, all sizes, me dad kept in his toolbox, so while everyone was out I sneaked in and helped myself. I tried and tried every one, but none would fit. In the meantime Rosie was still sorting the drawer over where she last put it, then all at once I heard her cry out, ''Ere it is, it was right at the back of the drawer beneath the knives an' forks.'

While I ran back home to put the keys back she already had the old piano open.

I was so excited now that I banged on those keys for all I was worth. Afterwards I opened up the piano stool and saw several faded pieces of music sheets. I took one out and tried

to read the notes, but it was all Chinese to me. The only thing
I could understand was it was a piece called 'Rock of Ages'.
Another was 'Abide with Me', and another was 'Onward
Christian Soldiers'.

I knew all these tunes off by heart, as we had sung them
many times in Sunday School and church. But I made believe.
I took each piece, propped it up on the music frame in front
of me and pretended to play from the music, and as I began
to play by ear I felt marvellous the way my fingers went over
those keys, but making plenty of mistakes when I struck the
dead ones. I was very excited, and so was Rosie – she even
called in some of the kids who were playing in the yard to
listen to me. But when the time for her mum to come home
drew near, Rosie locked up the piano and out we went to
wait. We were afraid the kids would tell on us, but Rosie said
if they did she wouldn't let them come in her house again.

But now I was getting fed up of trying to play the same old
tune, so one Saturday afternoon while Rosie's mum was out
I started practising again. I know it must have sounded awful
to some people, but I enjoyed it, so did Rosie and the kids. It
seemed that all the kids in the street came that day to try and
sing. But when they tried to dance they cried, 'Carn't yer
play summat else, we carn't dance ter that!'

After a few more tries I managed to hit the keys, and found
I could now play (after a fashion) 'Any Old Iron' and 'Knees
Up Mother Brown'. All the kids began to sing and dance
around the yard with Rosie. It was bedlam, with some kids
taking turns looking out for Rosie's mum to appear and to
warn us in time. But no one cared – even the 'looker-out'
joined in, which was a mistake. As soon as someone shouted
out that Mrs Pumfry was coming down the street the kids
scattered, leaving Rosie to run in and warn me. But before
she and I could close the lid, Mrs Pumfry almost fell into the
room.

'You wicked, wicked pair!' she yelled as she snatched up
the sheets of music and banged the lid down. I was trembling
now with fear, and so was Rosie. As tears ran down her
cheeks, her mother yelled again: 'An' what 'ave I told yer

about that piano! Never ter be opened! An' where did yer find the key?'

'In the back of the drawer, Mum,' whimpered Rosie.

'Well, in future it goes in my pocket. And as for you!' she added. 'I don't want ter see you in my 'ouse again! Now clear off!'

I didn't need telling twice. I fled.

I never did enter that house at number fifteen again, but Rosie and I were still friends.

When I told my mum later, she just scolded me and said that Rosie could come in our house any time. I was pleased about this, but it wasn't the same, for I loved any kind of musical instrument, and I vowed when I was old enough to get married the first thing I would buy would be a real piano.

But my big ideas never materialised until 1950, after my second marriage. Then I had two!

# The Facts of My Life

From the early age of three, I knew what I wanted from life. First, I wanted to grow up quickly and leave the god-forsaken place where I was born and lived with my parents and family. I wanted love and affection (which I never got from my parents). I wanted to be married and have lots of babies, to be rich and independent. But these hopes never turn out the way you wish when you're a child! When you reach middle age, or before, you often wish you were young again, and could do the things you had forgotten to do.

But no one can turn back the clock – although many would wish to. I know *I* don't, because *my* happiness is now, in my late years, and I have my independence. However, it wasn't until I was seventy-two years old and began to write the story of my life that I found *real* happiness and independence.

Looking back now and remembering those awful years, I know it was a mistake trying to grow up too soon.

I left school when I was fourteen, and started work. The older girls at the factory used to laugh and tell jokes about me because I wore stockings that were always falling down, old shoes that were much too big for me, and a short frock which had seen better days and showed my pink flannelette bloomers. I grew envious of how nice and tidy each of these young women looked, so after a few weeks I determined to leave.

Jobs were easy to find for young learners in my day, and with a few shillings I'd saved I made up my mind to go to the rag market in the Bull Ring and buy myself some cheap clothes to make myself look older, then get another job. I often smile to myself when I think about those years, and tell my grandchildren and great-grandchildren about my narrow escapes and the funnier side of my life.

I pinned my long black hair on top and put on a long hobble skirt, a bright-green blouse and a pair of second-hand high-heeled shoes, much too big for me. I also wore a pair of grey whalebone stays, which I had to pack with pieces of cotton waste to fill myself out. I really had no dress sense, but I thought I was the cat's whiskers.

On the way back from the Bull Ring market (which was then in Moat Row) I called at Snape's to buy Phul-Nana face powder and a lipstick. To make myself smell extra nice, I pushed the scented card Mr Snape gave me between my titties.

Often I tried to find hiding-places for my 'war paint', as Mum called my make-up, and when she did find it she put it on the fire. 'Only tarts an' cheap women use that stuff!' she would yell. 'An' if I find any mower, it'll goo on the bloody fire, an' yo with it!'

So I shared with Sally, the girl next door, but I always managed to wash my face clean in the brewhouse before I went indoors.

My parents and neighbours often said Sally was a bad girl, always seen with a different feller out late at night, yet I never saw any wrong in her. She was my friend, a little older than me, and always kind to me. Often we would arrange to meet each other on the Soho Road – called the 'Monkey Run' – where we would flirt with older boys. I had many narrow escapes trying to keep them at bay.

I was never told the facts of life, but I was a virgin until I was nearly eighteen. Then, in my foolish ignorance, I got myself pregnant and had to get married. That was in the Depression year 1921. I remember all those many years during my unhappy married life, it was hard for my husband to find employment. We had no real home, only my mother's attic, where we lived and slept six in a bed.

During the next ten years I had two miscarriages and five children, losing my eldest son as he came home from Nelson Street School – a shock I thought my husband and I would never get over. In 1931 my husband died and I was left with four young children to bring up, clothe and feed.

\* \* \*

Before my husband died, I had to turn my hand to anything to earn a few shillings to pay my mother rent and to buy food. Although sometimes my husband would leave a few shillings on the shelf when he sold bags of sawdust, more often than not he went out drinking. Often we quarrelled, but he never changed, and when he became bad-tempered the children and I kept out of his way.

One Saturday night my eldest sister Mary, who was a part-time barmaid at the Vine Tavern a few yards from where she lived in Carver Street, came to see me. Often she would bring me a glass of milk stout when my husband wasn't about, for he always objected to me having so much as one glass, or even going into a pub.

'I don't wanta see yer like yer mother!' he used to say.

I had bathed my children and put them to bed, and after I had put a patch on my little son's trousers, Mary arrived. When she asked if my husband was about, I said I didn't know where he was or when he'd be back. As she took the bottle of stout from her bag I got out a couple of glasses, and as I was drinking she said, 'Kate, would yer like to earn ten shillin'?'

'Ten shillin'? Are yer kiddin'?' I exclaimed.

'No, I ain't kiddin',' she replied, and began to smile.

When I asked what I had to do she said, 'There's an old white-haired couple comin' to the Vine tonight to celebrate their golden weddin', and the missus at the pub asked me if I knew anybody who could sing a few old songs for them and – '

'Why ask me?' I asked before she had time to finish.

'Well, the woman she engaged 'as let 'er down, and I mentioned you.'

'But Mary, I've never sung in a pub before, only when I was about ten years old when me dad sat me on the counter and I sang for his beer money. Any'ow, Charlie would kill me if I went an' he found out.'

'Charlie won't find out unless yer tell 'im, an' I know you ain't that daft! Any'ow, you'll only be away about an hour, you'll be back home in plenty of time before he returns. Knowin' 'im, he won't be back till they throw him out!'

'I'll think about it, Mary.'

'I must have me answer now, or she might get somebody else.'

'But I ain't even got a decent frock to wear!'

'That's no trouble, you can wear my blue taffeta one. It's too tight for me now, I know it will fit yer. So if you'll say you'll come, I'll give it yer.'

I always envied her that dress and ten shillings seemed a fortune to me in those days so, knowing I would be the owner of the blue taffeta dress, I agreed to go.

First I tiptoed up the attic stairs and, seeing that my children were fast asleep, tiptoed down again.

Mary had already got the curling irons in the fire for my hair, and after she had brought in the dress and I slipped it on she put a little powder on my face and neck. As she made my lips up with her lipstick, she said, 'Now look at yerself in the mirror.'

I couldn't believe my eyes – how different I looked, and what an improvement on my old blouse and skirt that I had to wear all the time and wash weekly to try to make myself look presentable wherever I went!

As I stood admiring myself, I heard my sister say, 'Why, yer look ten years younger. Anyway, if yer stand admiring yerself much longer you'll crack the mirror.'

Then we both laughed.

Before we left the house I listened once again at the bottom of the attic stairs, satisfied that all was quiet. We made our way towards the Vine. I was still very timid, but my sister put her arm in mine and said I would be OK once I got inside the smoke room. I felt as if everyone's eyes were on me as I looked around. In the far corner was a long table with all kinds of eats laid out, and bunches of flowers. I was told later that evening that kind neighbours had had a door-to-door collection for Mr and Mrs Wright's anniversary. In another corner of the room was an upright piano – its lid was open and as I looked at it I thought: I hope it plays better than the one I tried to practise on when I was a young girl.

Flo, as everyone called the missus of the pub, was no

stranger to me; often she used to serve me in the Bottle and Jug Department when I fetched my dad's beer. She was a small dumpy woman with black frizzy hair which came down to her shoulders. To me she always seemed overdressed, and that night she wore a long flowing red velvet dress, long red dangling earrings, several rows of different-coloured beads and several rings on her fingers.

I thought, too, that she wouldn't have looked so loud if she hadn't had too much war paint on her face and lips. But as the missus of the pub, I supposed she had to look and be different to the rest of her customers. As she walked towards me and put her arm round my shoulders she said, 'I'm glad you could come, my dear, your sister has told me all about you. So sit down, and don't look so nervous.'

Suddenly I heard Mary say, 'She won't afta stop long, Flo, as soon as she's sung a couple of numbers I'll 'ave to go 'ome with 'er before 'er 'usband comes back.'

'Very well,' replied Flo as she turned to me again. 'Now, sit yourself down. We're not ready to begin yet, so would you like a drink? Whisky or gin, or – '

'Oh, no, no, thank you,' I answered quickly. 'But I would like a glass of stout.'

The old barman brought over the glass of stout and a gin for Mary, who was to accompany me at the piano.

While I was waiting to be announced, I still felt nervous, for I'd never sung in front of a lot of people before. But after another couple of stouts and a sip of Mary's gin I had plenty of Dutch courage to sing my numbers.

I knew I had a good singing voice. When I followed my sister towards the piano and she started to play, everybody in the room applauded. Then, when it was my turn to sing, I sang my favourite, 'Home Sweet Home', which was the song I learnt at school. Everybody applauded for the second time. I felt then that I could have gone on singing all night. But as I walked away from the piano, the old white-haired gentleman came towards me and asked if I would sing again.

'That was lovely, me wench, but could you please sing "When Your Hair Has Turned to Silver" for me an' me wife?'

he asked. I stood beside the piano again and as Mary struck the first notes, I began to sing:

> 'When your hair has turned to silver,
> I will love you just the same.
> I will always call you sweetheart,
> That will always be your name.
> Through a garden filled with roses,
> Down a sunset trail we'll stray.
> When your hair has turned to silver,
> I will love you as today.'

I don't know how I sounded, for all the time I was singing tears filled my eyes as I saw the white-haired old couple kiss and embrace like a pair of young lovers. The applause was deafening – not only for me but for the old couple, who were still hugging each other.

'Mary,' I managed to whisper, 'it's getting late, I'll have to go.'

'Can't you stop an' do another number?' she asked.

'No! Yer know I've got ter get back 'ome, I've stayed too long as it is.' I didn't stay even for a sandwich.

'Oh, all right. I'll go over an' speak to Flo.'

But the missus was already walking towards me with a large bunch of flowers and the ten-shilling note. As she gave them to me she asked if I would come again.

'I'll 'ave to think about it,' I replied. 'But I'll let my sister know.'

She thanked me again and as Mary and I walked out into the street I put the ten-shilling note down inside my frock and, hugging those lovely flowers to me, I said, 'Mary, I think you better have these flowers, or me 'usband or me mum will start askin' questions an' I wouldn't know what to say. Any'ow,' I added, 'I've got what I want and the money will come in useful.'

But while we were laughing and saying what a wonderful night we'd had, I happened to glance across the street.

Suddenly I stood there scared, as I saw my husband standing beneath the light of the street lamp watching me.

'Kate,' I heard my sister say, 'don't be scared. I'll come 'ome with yer an' explain.'

But there was no time. Before we got a few steps further he suddenly dashed across the road. The next thing I knew, he snatched the flowers out of my arms and threw them across the street, then as he struck me across my face I saw stars, then as he tore the frock almost from my back I called out for my sister, but she had already fled.

Crowds were now gathering around, and as he turned to answer some of the women who were yelling at him I saw my chance and ran home.

But there was Mum, sitting by the fire ready to greet me. 'Serves you bloody well right, an' I 'ope 'e gives yer some mower!' she cried out when she saw my eyes swollen and my lovely frock all torn.

'But I've done no 'arm,' I began to whimper. 'I was only singin' an' I needed the money.'

'But yer know 'e's ferbid yer gooin' in a pub!'

I knew it was useless to try to explain to her, or to expect any help. So I went upstairs, and as I sat on the foot of the bed weeping, I heard Charlie come up. I was now scared stiff, expecting him to give me a belting. But when he pulled me up off the bed and saw what he had done, he just said he was sorry and walked back down the stairs. I didn't see him until the early hours of the next morning. Then he took me in his arms and said again how sorry he was for what he'd done.

After that, he began to change. He found a part-time job in a tatter's yard sorting out old clothes and pieces of copper, brass and iron. Things began to get smoother, but after a few weeks he kept coming home feeling sick. One morning he collapsed. I ran for the doctor and when he came and examined Charlie, he said he would have to go into hospital. But he was stubborn and refused to go. Eventually his pains got worse. I didn't know what to do, as I was expecting my fifth baby any day. Then a couple of days later, when I came home from work and saw an ambulance outside the house, I knew the worst.

Charlie was taken to Hallam Street Hospital, where he died of a perforated gastric ulcer. That same night I gave birth to my baby daughter, whom I later christened Mary, after my sister.

That was the 22nd of April 1931. My husband was only thirty and I was only twenty-eight, left penniless with four young children to care for and a drunken mother to contend with.

Now that I was left a destitute widow with no pension but four young dependants, I tried going out cleaning – I even got a part-time job in a jam factory. But that didn't last long – I got the sack for eating the strawberries and bringing some home for the children. When I did eventually find a job working on a heavy press, my mum wanted half my pay to look after her grandchildren. But when I came home unexpectedly one afternoon, I found my youngest baby still lying in her cot with her nappy caked hard to her bottom. I was livid to see how she had been neglected. I picked her up, bathed her and gave her a feed, cleaned the cot out, and after asking one of my neighbours to keep an eye on her, I went to find my mother. I didn't have to look – I was told she was in a neighbour's house round the back yard.

I knew my mother drank, but I never expected to see her drunk. There was a gramophone playing and I could hear singing when I knocked on the door of number seventeen. No one heard my knock, so I kicked the door for all I was worth. Suddenly an old man opened it. 'Who yer want?' I heard him splutter.

'Tell my mother to come out now!' I shouted through the open door.

'Sod orf, yer mother ain't 'ere!'

'I know she's in there, I've been told! And I ain't going till she comes out, or she'll be sorry.'

Neighbours gathered outside the door when they heard me

shouting. I was about to call out again when Mum stumbled out, looking all fuddled with drink. As the door slammed behind her I cried out for all the neighbours to hear, 'You drunken sot! Leavin' my babby all day lying in her cot all caked in her mess! An' you takin' me money to look after her! You should be ashamed of yerself!'

Suddenly she raised her hand to strike me, but she was too fuddled even to see where she was. I went back down the yard, and as soon as I had collected my baby from Mrs Taylor I went indoors and found my mother lying stretched out on the sofa fast asleep.

She had never been like this when my dad was alive – how I wished he'd been there that day!

The next morning when I sent my other two children to school, I asked Mrs Taylor if she would look after Jean and Mary while I went to work. When she refused, I told her I would pay her the same as I had always given my mum.

'It ain't the money, Kate – God knows I could do with it! But yer know what yer mum's like, she'd 'ave the 'ole street up in arms, sayin' I took 'er job off 'er, an' them bein' 'er grandchildren an' all.'

'Do some of you neighbours good ter stand up to 'er! Yer seem to let 'er get away with everything!' I replied angrily.

'I don't know why *you* can't 'old yer own to 'er,' she exclaimed, 'instead of come bawlin' ter me.'

'I'm sorry to lose me temper. I understand, and I wish I could, Mrs Taylor, but livin' with 'er is different, and I 'ave to curb me tongue at times, otherwise she'd turn me an' my children out. Then where would we go? Anyway,' I added, 'I've got other plans now, I'll go to the parish an' let them keep us.'

But what little they gave us wasn't enough even to feed one hungry mouth, let alone five of us.

# A Bitter Struggle

During the following months I tried to struggle on, with only parish relief and the firewood I was selling from door to door. Often it would be late at night before I could call at the little local shop in Albion Street and buy food. One night, after feeding my children and putting them to bed, I started to gather up their dirty underclothes ready for the brewhouse the next day, then I saw my son tossing and turning in his sleep. As we slept five in a bed, I tried to calm him down in case he woke his sisters up. But as soon as I felt his forehead, I knew at once he was sickening for something. I crept quietly down the attic stairs and as I came back with a bowl of cool water and a flannel, I heard my mother shout from her bedroom.

'Wot are yer doin' up this time a mornin'?'

'John's feverish,' I replied. 'An' I'll 'aveta get the doctor to 'im in the mornin'.'

As she came out on to the landing she said, 'I 'eard yer up an' down, carn't sleep meself with this stiflin' bloody weather,' and closed the bedroom door.

As soon as I went up the attic stairs I saw John sitting up in bed with his eyes wide open.

'Mum, I'm thirsty an' I feel 'ot.'

'Please God,' I said to myself, 'don't let him be ill.'

I gave him a drink of my home-made ginger beer, then took off his little shirt, sponged his naked body and looked for any spots, but there were none to be seen. I lay down beside him until he went to sleep, and stayed awake in case he got worse.

Just as dawn broke I was looking through the attic window, which I had propped open with a brick, when I heard my mum moving about. I was hoping she would come up to look at John, but I heard her go downstairs. Later that morning I woke my three girls, and after washing them and getting Kathleen ready for school, I took Jean and Mary to our next-door neighbour to keep an eye on them while I went for the doctor. But as soon as I went back indoors my mother cried, 'I don't know why yer wanta doctor, I don't believe in 'em, they kill more kids than they can cure. Any'ow,' she added, 'give 'im a dose of castor oil, it's betta than all yer doctors give yer, an' while yer think about it, if yer can afford a doctor, don't forget I want me rent!'

All I had in my purse that day was 6s. 6d., but I ignored her – whatever happened she could wait for her rent.

I slung my coat over my shoulder and ran for the doctor. Dr McKenzie, the local doctor, lived only two streets away.

Luckily for me, I was first to arrive at his small surgery. As soon as I explained what was wrong, he said he would call in an hour's time and to keep John warm.

When I arrived back, I was met by one of the neighbours who said my mother was in the brewhouse chatting. But I wasn't interested in where she was or what she did – at times I felt I hated her.

As soon as I entered the attic I noticed my son was still asleep but didn't look so flushed.

I took Mary and Jean towards the small fireplace and washed and fed them, and while they sat on the mat playing with little blocks of wood I sponged John down again and made him comfortable, while I waited for the doctor.

When Dr McKenzie came and examined my son, he asked if any of my other children had had measles or chickenpox.

'Only measles, Doctor,' I replied anxiously.

After examining John for the second time, he said, 'I can't see any spots, or a rash.'

'But what is wrong with him, Doctor?' I asked anxiously.

'I believe he's labouring under a nervous fever,' he replied. 'I'll give you a prescription to take to my surgery, where my wife will make up a bottle of medicine. Give him a teaspoon three times a day, then when he's finished the dose bring him to see me.' Just as he was writing out the slip of paper, I saw my mother enter the room.

'Wot's wrong with 'im?' she cried.

'Just a feverish cold, but he'll be all right in a day or two,' the doctor replied.

'I don't know why 'er sent fer yo! I could 'ave gid 'im summat betta than yo alwis prescribe!' bawled Mum.

Suddenly Dr McKenzie turned to face her. I saw his face go red as he shouted, 'Leave the room at once! If I need your advice, I'll call you!'

As he turned his back on Mum and gave me the slip of paper, I saw her leave, and as she went down the stairs I heard her mumble, 'It's my 'ouse an' nobody tells me when or wot ter doo!'

As soon as we heard the door slam behind her, I offered the doctor his five-shilling fee for the visit and the medicine, but to my surprise he refused to take it.

'You need it more. Buy some milk for the little ones. But', he added, 'don't tell my other patients, otherwise no one will want to pay.'

''E will get better soon, Doctor?' I asked as I thanked him.

'Yes, with care. But that fever is due to this unwholesome air and this damn place, and unless you can find a healthier place for you and your children, they'll never grow up strong.'

I thanked him again, and after I had fetched the medicine I sat down and wept. The doctor's words had alarmed me. Where were we to go? I'd tried for years to move from this vile place, but who would take me and four young children when everybody in the district was overcrowded?

I had even asked my married sisters and brothers to take them into their homes until I could go out to work and save enough money to rent a house or other rooms, but with no result. I still remember their answers: 'Sorry, but we don't 'ave the room. 'Ow can we look after them when we 'ave ter goo out ter work?'

I was now both destitute and desperate.

Several weeks later things began to get worse. People didn't want to buy smelly fishboxes for firewood. I could no longer see any future ahead for me and my children.

I tried hard to claim a widow's pension (which was then only ten shillings a week) but I was refused – there weren't enough stamps on my husband's insurance card – neither could I claim any sick pay (or panel money). There were no social services in those days, nor citizens' advice bureaux, nor children's allowances. There wasn't even the Pill, only back-street abortion. But I was scared. I'd heard of girls being found out and prosecuted, or even dying. I was left with a means test or parish relief. Like many others in similar circumstances I did odd jobs on the sly to help feed our children. But if we were found out, we were brought before the tribunal and got nothing. The only help I got was boots and clothes from the *Daily Mail* Fund. But you couldn't eat these, or try pawning them. We were almost starving, and when I saw my children begging for food outside the same factory gates I had begged at as a child, I was heartbroken. I didn't want them to grow up as I had been dragged up.

There was only one heartbreaking decision: I had to let my children go into a Dr Barnardo's Home, until I could leave that bug-infested attic and find work and rent a house for them to come home to.

I worked hard night and day and got a home together. Then eventually, after eight years, I succeeded in getting them back to Birmingham, but they were no longer babies. Mary was nine years old, no longer the baby I knew. Jean was twelve, Kathleen was fourteen and my son John was fifteen. John was sent into the navy before I could get him home, and was on the high seas in many major battles during the war. Not until my daughters came home did they tell me how cruelly and harshly they were treated, yet how different those Homes are in this day and age!

But I knew that if I hadn't persevered to get them away from there, they would have been shipped off to Canada, and I might never have seen them again.

I often wonder if people of this generation who read my books condemn me for parting with my children. Let them think again. What would they have done in my place?

If we had stayed in that godforsaken hole in Camden Drive, my children and I would not be what we are today.

# Turning Point

The day I left my children at Dr Barnardo's I had only about eight shillings in my pocket. I decided it was now time to make a break from that unlucky attic and my mother's house.

It was a bitterly cold day when I finally pushed a few clean underclothes into a brown paper bag, and with the shabby clothes I stood up in I walked from that house and vowed never to return. As I went down the yard I saw several little children with whom my children had once played games – some younger ones sitting on the cold steps sucking their dirty dummies, others fighting and swearing as their mothers stood gossiping with folded arms.

I gazed around for the last time and thanked the Lord that my children were away from all this squalor. I had no idea where I was going until I found myself opposite the gates of Warstone Lane Cemetery, where my brother Frank, his wife Nellie and their family lived in an open yard, in a one-room-down-and-one-up old house similar to my mother's.

I had no intention of calling on them, but crossed the road and went through the cemetery gates. I sat down on a stone bench, then I saw, coming slowly along the gravel path, our old Vicar Smith walking in front of someone's coffin, carried by six bearers. I began to weep when I remembered my son Charles, and his father, my husband, buried here under the earth with no headstone to say who they were or where. Suddenly I began to feel tired, and I closed my eyes. I must have dozed off.

Now, I don't believe in supernatural powers or ghosts, yet I heard a voice whisper, 'Don't sit here in this morbid place feeling sorry for yourself. Leave now and speak to your brother.'

Suddenly I began to feel shivers going through me. I

thought: was it my husband's voice I heard? Or have I been dreaming? Yet the voice was so real.

I got up off the bench. The next thing I did was to cross the road. When my brother opened his door, he was surprised to see me. He greeted me with open arms, and so did Nellie.

I still recall that wonderful warm greeting, as they made me sit by the fire. As soon as Nellie had given me a hot cup of tea, she asked me why I had come to see them.

I explained about the voice I'd heard, and my brother began to laugh: 'Yer musta bin dreamin'.'

'Don't laugh, Frank. It was no dream,' I replied seriously. 'I'm sure it was my 'usband's voice I 'eard.'

'You remind me of Mum with your superstitions,' replied Frank, still smiling.

'Don't yer mention yer mother in this 'ouse, Frank!' Nellie piped up. 'Anyway, Kate,' she added as she turned to me, 'we've already 'eard the gossip, an' we know 'ow yer feelings are.'

'I had to do it, Nellie, there was no other alternative I could think of,' I replied as I thought of my children so very far away from me.

'We understand, don't we, Frank?' said Nellie.

'Yes, Kate. I'm sorry to hear what 'as 'appened,' my brother replied. 'Now dry yer eyes an' after yo've thawed out we'll get yer a bitta supper.'

As soon as my brother left the room Nellie said, 'I'm sorry too, Kate, and if we could 'ave 'elped yer we would 'ave. It's a pity you 'ad ter live there, I'm glad me an' Frank dain't goo when yer mum asked us. Although this place ain't much, it's our 'ome, an' we're 'appy, an' if yer like ter mek shift sleepin' on the sofa, yer welcome ter stay until yer find summat betta.'

'Thanks, Nellie, but I've got ter find a place ter live and find work so that I can get me children back.'

'I understand,' I heard her reply as she went into the small kitchen.

After my first meal since the day before, Frank began to

make me up a bed on the sofa. But Nellie would insist that my brother could sleep there and I could share her bed.

My sister-in-law said I could go up when I was ready, and I went after thanking them for letting me stay and wishing them both good night. Later she came up with a stone hot-water bottle to make me comfortable.

It wasn't long before I fell into a restless sleep. I didn't feel Nellie get in beside me, nor did I hear her get up the next morning.

It was late when I awoke. I guessed they had both decided to let me sleep on. As I got out of bed and began to dress I glanced at myself in the wardrobe mirror, and noticed how sallow my face was. My eyes too looked and felt tired; even my mouth was drooping at the corners. My hands were rough and chapped and my fingernails were broken and dirty.

I knew then that if I was to get a job or lodgings I had to clean and smarten myself up a bit.

As soon as I went downstairs, I washed myself at the sink. Then, after breakfast, I helped Nellie with the washing-up. My brother was already getting ready to go to work when I said I too would have to be looking for work, also lodgings. When he asked me what I was doing about money, I told him I still had a few shillings.

'But that ain't gonna tek yer far!' he exclaimed. 'Yer betta tek this two quid.'

As he pushed the two gold sovereigns into my hand, I cried, 'No, Frank, you'll need it yerself. Any'ow I don't know when I'll be able ter pay yer back.'

'Tek it,' Nellie replied. 'An' get yer 'air done an' a bit of paint an' powder on yer face, an' yer can leave that ragged coat yer wearin'. There's one of mine upstairs in the closet, it's better than yours.'

I felt very tearful, for they were so kind to me. I also knew that if they had had room I could have stayed. But I was too near Camden Drive and its sordid surroundings and too many sad memories. I knew that if I was to make a future for my children and myself, I had to make a move as soon as possible. I thanked them both for their kindness and promised that as soon as I got on my feet I would come and see them again. And wearing Nellie's good coat, I carried the brown paper bag which still held my clean underclothes and a few sandwiches she had put inside. I made my way down the yard, but they both insisted they should come and see me to the corner of Vyse Street, where I was to wait for the Lodge Road tram. As we stood waiting we kissed each other goodbye, and as the tram slowly came up Warstone Lane and stopped near Chamberlain's clock, I felt sad that I had to leave them.

As soon as I had boarded the tram and we waved to each other, I heard my brother call out, 'Best of luck, Kate, an' don't ferget if yer need us, yer know where we live.'

I still remember those words and the tears in their eyes as they waved.

I got on top of the tram and when I had found an empty seat and the conductor had taken my fare, I began to weep again. All I had in the world was the two sovereigns and eight shillings, and the contents of the paper bag.

As I got off that tram in Edmund Street, I began to plan what I was going to do.

That day, in the late autumn of 1931, was the turning point of my life.

As I walked along Edmund Street and down Colemore Row and made my way towards the Bull Ring, I stopped to look in several stores and shop windows. And as I admired all the pretty dresses, shoes and other brand-new garments, I almost said aloud, 'One day I'm going to be able to buy some of those, not left-off garments from the rag market' – where I was now heading.

Little did I realise that in the years ahead I would be independent, have money in the bank and a small business. But I had many worries and heartaches, too, in those years.

As soon as I was inside the rag market, which was then in Moat Row, I looked around at each stall to see what I could buy. What I needed now was a cheap second-hand frock or a blouse and skirt, a pair of shoes and a hat. On one of the stalls I went to I happened to see a pretty blue taffeta dress. It looked similar to the one my sister had given me. I nearly bought it, but I changed my mind. It would have reminded me too often of the night my husband tore it from my back.

I went to the next stall and saw, hanging from the rail, a good second-hand dress. It was navy-blue serge with a white lace collar and cuffs. It also had pearl buttons down the front. On the stall lay a pair of patent shoes and a blue pillbox hat with a veil. I knew if I bought it it wouldn't leave me much change in my purse for other things.

The frock was marked 12s. 6d., the shoes 5s. 6d., and the hat 3s. 6d. Plucking up courage, I asked the old woman who owned the stall if she would take a little less.

'I'm sorry, me dear,' I heard her mumble. 'I bin sittin' 'ere all mornin' freezin', an' I ain't bin able ter sell a thing! So yer betta try somewhere else! Any'ow me clothes are better-quality than the others they sell on their stalls,' she added.

'P'raps yer prices are too 'igh,' I replied as I walked towards the next stall.

As I was still looking for something cheaper, I hoped she'd remember what I said and call me back. She did.

'Come on, dearie,' I heard her call out, 'I've changed me mind. I wanta get 'ome early any'ow, an' I can see yer in need of 'em. So what if I let yer 'ave 'em a bit cheaper without the 'at?'

I didn't need the hat anyway, for I had made up my mind to have my hair bobbed and marcel waved. She knocked a shilling off the frock and sixpence off the shoes. I still had a bargain.

I paid her the 16s. 6d., put the clothes in the brown paper carrier with my clean shift bloomers, underskirt and stockings, and thanked her. Then as I walked away she called out to me, ''Ere yar, dearie, I'll give yer the 'at.'

'Thank you,' I replied, 'but I won't need it. I'm gooin' to 'ave me 'air cut.'

'Well, yer can 'ave it any'ow, it might come in useful one day. An' I'm closin' me stall anyway.'

I took the hat and thanked her again, then I heard her call

out, 'Don't forget ter come agen, dearie, you'll alwis get a bargin orf old Aggie.'

I began to smile. I hoped not. I hoped one day I would be in a better position to rig myself out in new clothes, not somebody's cast-offs.

As soon as I came out of the rag market, it began to rain. I thought: that pillbox hat will come in useful after all. When I took it out of the bag and placed it on my head, I realised it was too large and fell over my eyes. I didn't intend to carry it about with me. Then, just as I thought of throwing it over somebody's wall, I happened to see an old woman standing on the pavement trying to sell flowers.

She only had a shabby black shawl round her shoulders and I noticed that she wasn't wearing anything on her head. As I took the hat from my carrier, I walked across the road towards her.

''Ere you are, Gran'ma, put this on yer 'ead, it's too big for me,' I said.

'Oh thank yer, luv,' she replied. 'But would yer like ter buy a bunch of flowers from me?'

'Sorry, Gran'ma, but I wouldn't know what ter do with them.'

But as I felt sorry for her standing and calling the price of her flowers in that pouring rain, I opened my purse and gave her sixpence. She thanked me. Then as I walked away, I looked back to see that she was wearing that pillbox hat.

The rain began to ease off, although there was still a cold wind. I was glad when the sun came out.

I then made my way towards Northwood Street public baths, paid my threepence for a tablet of soap and the loan of a corporation towel and made my way towards the cubicle, and while I lay soaking myself in that hot soapy water, I remembered the last time I was there. It was many years before, when our schoolteacher took us once a week – it was only one penny then. And I hadn't had a good soaking since. It was always a wash-down in the copper boiler, in the communal brewhouse, or the zinc bath in front of the fire on Friday nights.

As I lay there that day, I felt I could have soaked myself for hours, until I heard the attendant shout through the door, 'You in theea! Are yer all right?'

'Yes,' I replied.

'Well, 'urry yerself! Yer can't stay in there all day! Somebody else is waitin' to get in!'

I dried myself quickly and changed into my clean underclothes. I put on my stockings and the frock and shoes I'd bought, and after putting my old dirty clothes I didn't want into the brown paper bag I felt clean and refreshed.

As I handed the wet towel over to the attendant she cried as she snatched it from me, 'Next time yo come, Mrs, I'll time yer!'

I didn't stop to answer, but smiled to myself as I thought: I hope there won't be a next time I have to go to public baths.

I still carried the bag with my dirty old undergarments in, also my old frock and well-worn-down shoes. I didn't need them any longer, yet I couldn't carry them about with me. I had to get rid of them somehow.

As soon as I heard the rag-and-bone man coming down the street I dropped them in the gutter for him to collect, and hurried away.

My next call was at a small-fronted shop, which said haircutting and waving. But when I walked in the woman said I had to make an appointment, which was in an hour's time, and the cost was 4s. 6d. for a cut, shampoo and marcel waves. I paid a 1s. deposit and told her I would come back in an hour.

As I walked around to kill time I came to a little house where they sold home-made cakes and tea. I went in and bought a cup of tea, then I realised I felt hungry. But when I felt in my paper bag for the sandwiches Nellie had put in, I realised I must have left them amongst the garments I'd dumped in the gutter. I bought another cup of tea and a plate of cakes, and then it was time to have my hair done.

It was the first time I had ever had my hair done professionally and when I was finished and stood up to look in the mirror, I couldn't believe it was me. I felt flattered. My hair had been cut below my ears and marcel waved with hot iron crimpers, which looked like large paper clips. I thought I looked like one of the flappers you saw in advertisements. That style was all the rage then.

Although I had only about a pound left in my purse, I was glad I'd had my hair done, and now my next move was to find somewhere to sleep for the night.

# *Ellen*

I knew if I went back to my brother and his wife they would gladly give me shelter. But I also knew I wouldn't get anywhere if I changed my mind, and I couldn't take advantage of their kindness. It was now late in the afternoon, and it began to get chilly. I wrapped my coat closer around me, and as I walked along Great Hampton Street looking to see if there were any rooms to let, I happened to see a notice in a newpaper-shop window, advertising a room. But when I hurried inside and asked, I was told it was already taken.

Further down the street I came to a little tea shop. I was about to buy myself a cup when I saw another notice: 'Furnished room to let, suit young lady or gentleman'. I almost fell inside that tea shop. There were several customers waiting to be served. The woman behind the counter didn't look very pleased when I cried, 'Could yer please tell me if that room's been taken what's advertised in the winda?'

'Yo'll afta wait yer turn, I got customers ter serve!'

'But I must know now,' I replied eagerly. 'Will yer write the address down? I 'aven't got a pencil,' I added as I stared at her.

'Yo'll afta wait!' she shouted again as she went on serving a customer.

I nearly yelled 'Grumpy old bugger!' But I knew that wouldn't get me anywhere.

I began to tap my fingers impatiently on the counter, then I saw a young man take a pencil from his pocket.

'Now come on, Maggie, let's have it,' he said pleasantly.

''Er won't get it, a young feller come arfta it an hour agoo.'

'But it might not be suited for 'im – I can try!' I replied.

'It's 5A Soho Road,' she snapped. ''Er name's Mrs 'Ands.'

As the young man gave me the name and address he smiled

and whispered, 'Old Maggie must have got out the wrong side of the bed and forgot to take her little liver pills. Anyway, dear, good luck.'

I thanked him and ran out of the shop and down the street towards Soho Road. I knew the road from years before when we teenagers used to call it the Monkey Run – we did our flirting there. Yet I never knew then where number 5A was. Up one side of the street and down the other I hurried, but still I couldn't find it. I was now cold and hungry, and the cheap shoes I bought that day were beginning to pinch my toes.

'If I don't find it soon,' I said to myself, 'there's only one alternative: I'll have to state my case at the Kenyon Street police station and ask the inspector to give me shelter for the night.'

I was just about to despair when I saw, a few feet away, five small houses which lay almost hidden in a cul-de-sac, and there was number 5A at the end. Each house, I could see, had two rooms up and down, each house was painted brown and cream, and each house looked the same, only there were clean white lace curtains at their windows, draped differently. Everywhere looked fresh and clean, even the narrow pavement. I hurried to the end house and lifted the bright brass lion's-head knocker, but there was no answer. I tried again, only louder. Soon I saw a woman peep her head round the door. When she saw me standing on the step, she opened the door wider.

She was rather a tall, upright woman with greying hair, wearing a long brown leg-o'-mutton-sleeve dress that almost hid her feet. She wore no jewellery, only a fob watch pinned to her chest. As I looked up at her I thought she looked severe. This made me feel very nervous, but just as my courage began to desert me I saw her smile as she asked, 'Have you come about the room?'

'Er ... er ... yes,' I stammered. 'I've bin sent by the woman from the ... er ... tea shop.'

'Oh yes, Maggie,' she replied, smiling. 'Everybody knows

Maggie – her bark's worse than her bite; she's a good old soul really. Anyway, you better come in out of the cold.'

As I followed her through the narrow hall I noticed two rooms, one each side of the hall, and stairs led off the kitchen, where I saw a blazing fire roaring in a bright black-leaded range. I couldn't resist walking up to it to warm my hands. She told me to draw up a chair and sit by the fire, and while she went into the scullery to make a cup of tea I gazed round the room. There were several framed pictures of scenes on the walls and photos in silver frames on the mantelshelf, an old dresser with odd crocks that might have been antique. There was also an oval polished table, four leather chairs and an armchair, and a threadbare rug. Everything in the room was old and well-worn, but highly polished and clean. I couldn't see a bit of dust anywhere, only the few ashes in the hearth.

As I sat looking around the woman came in with two cups of tea on a tray and half a dozen biscuits.

'As soon as you've drunk your tea and had a warm, I'll show you the room,' she said pleasantly.

'Then it's not been taken by the young man Maggie said she'd sent?'

'No, he wasn't suitable.'

I didn't ask why in case she thought I was being too nosy, but I did ask how much the room was.

'You must see it first, dear, then we can come to some agreement.'

No more was said until we had drunk our tea and eaten our biscuits.

I followed her up the threadbare carpeted stairs – I counted eleven – and on each side of the landing was a bedroom.

As she walked into the one on the left, I followed. She turned and said, 'There isn't much furniture, but it's clean and comfortable. I'll leave you to look around, and when you come downstairs you can let me know what you decide about the rent.'

Before I could answer she was gone.

Although the room was scantily furnished, it seemed a

palace to what I had left behind. There was a single bed with brass rails and well-patched clean bedcovers and a pillowslip with embroidered pansies on the corner, a tall oak wardrobe, a marble-topped dressing- and wash-stand with a crock bowl and a jug, a towel and a piece of soap, a wicker chair beside the bed and a hand-pegged rag rug beside the small fireplace. The rest of the floor was well-scrubbed bare boards. The walls were bare, but there was no sign of bugs. Everything was old but clean.

Thousands of people would have turned their nose up at this, but to me it was heaven.

After looking in the wardrobe I looked under the bed where I saw what I expected to see, the crock po.

When I went downstairs to tell the woman I would take it, I saw her sitting by the fire with an open Bible. As I entered she looked up and asked if the room was suitable.

'Yes, thank you,' I replied, 'but I would like ter know 'ow much yer askin' for the rent.'

'It's 7s. 6d. a week bed and breakfast, but other meals you will have to buy out unless you wish to have supper in, then you will have to put a few coppers in the meter. That will be a week in advance, dear.'

'Thank you, Mrs Hands,' I replied.

'Now sit down and tell me your name.'

As I opened up my purse and gave her three half-crowns, I told her my name was Mrs Flood and I was a widow. I hoped she wouldn't ask too many questions in case she changed her mind about letting the room. But when she said I looked too young to be a widow I told her it was a long story, and that I would tell her about my life and where my children were. But this was not the time or the place, and I was pleased she didn't ask, for I didn't feel I wanted her pity, otherwise I would have broken down and wept.

'When can I move in?' I asked quickly, hoping she would say now.

'As soon as you wish, dear,' she replied.

'I would like to stay tonight if yer wouldn't mind.'

'But you haven't brought any luggage with you – why do you wish to stay?'

'Me an' me mum had a big row and I walked out an' left an' I said I'd never go back there agen, that's why I was lookin' for a room ter stay.'

As soon as she saw my tears she said, 'Very well, dear, you can bring your luggage tomorrow. But what about your nightdress? Anyway,' she added, 'you may borrow one of mine tonight.'

After thanking her I said, 'Do yer mind if I go up to bed now, Mrs Hands? I'm so tired.'

'Very well, dear, but first I'll fill you a bottle to put in your bed.'

As she handed me the stone bottle filled with hot water and the long pink flannel nightdress, I could have broken down and wept. I had never known such kindness. As she sat down in her chair she opened up the Bible again then, turning to me, she whispered, 'Good night and God bless you, my dear.'

'Good night, Mrs Hands, and thank you,' I managed to answer.

As soon as I had kicked my shoes off I sat on the side of that bed and wept. Thinking about my children, I imagined that now they would be tucked up in bed and fast asleep. I hoped and prayed that they were clothed and well fed and didn't miss me too much, and that soon we would be together again. After asking God to take extra care of my children, I got undressed, slipped the flannel nightie on and lay down to think about tomorrow.

I now had only a few shillings left in my purse. I knew I had to buy a nightdress and a few extra clothes – any old things, even if I didn't wear them – before I could get a job.

I lay down planning what I intended to do until I fell into a restless sleep. When I awoke the next morning I saw that all the bedclothes had slipped on to the floor. I got out of bed, washed in the basin, and when I was dressed I went downstairs.

In the kitchen I saw my landlady frying bacon on the fire.

As soon as she saw me she said, 'Good morning, dear, did you sleep well?'

'Yes,' I replied. 'But I must have been a bit restless during the night.'

'It often happens the first time in a strange bed. Anyway,' she added, 'you may wash at the sink in the scullery, and while I finish cooking breakfast you will find the lavatory through the scullery door and down the yard.'

She had her own private back yard, with a small wash-house with a copper boiler and a wooden mangle, and next to the wash-house I saw the lavatory, all whitewashed, old but clean. Although it had a square wooden seat it also had a long iron chain to flush water. It wasn't like the dry communal closets we shared where we used to live. And as I sat there that morning, I remembered that was the only place I could try to educate myself with my dictionary, away from my mum and sisters and brothers, who always criticised me for what they said was a waste of time.

My dictionary helped me to talk a lot better, but I still drop my aitches and when I get excited or lose my temper I still come out with the 'Brummie' accent.

After breakfast I helped to wash up the greasy dishes, then went up to make my bed. When I came down the stairs my landlady was sitting with the Bible on her lap.

'I'll 'ave to be off now, Mrs Hands, I'll be back later tonight.'

'I think you may call me Ellen,' she replied.

'Thank you, Ellen, and my name's Kate.'

'Very well, Kate,' she answered, smiling across the room at me.

I felt so pleased that I had found such a kind and friendly person, I felt like throwing my arms around her and kissing her, but I didn't want to seem too familiar.

# Into Business

As I walked down the street I made my way to town and the rag market again. I knew that I had only a few shillings left. The first things I had to get were a nightdress and a few undergarments, until I could find work and buy better. I was looking around for the cheapest stall when I saw old Aggie pop her head around beneath a pile of old clothes. "Ello me dear, come ter buy yerself some of me old clothes agen?' she called.

'Sorry, Aggie, yer too dear, I'm lookin' for something cheaper.' As I walked away I heard her shout, 'Goo ter the others, then, but yer won't get nothin' cheaper or better! They'll do yer, you'll see!'

I began to smile to myself as I crossed over to another stall, where I found what I wanted. The garments were old but looked clean – anyway, I would ask Ellen later if I could wash them. Now, with only a few coppers left, I had to find work.

I walked up one street and down another, carrying my garments in a paper carrier. I was getting tired and hungry, but I had to find a job.

Before and during my married life I had worked at several firms learning enamelling and polishing motor plates, badges, also jewellery. I was an experienced enameller, but I didn't want to go to the firms where I had learnt my trade. Although many of the people I used to work with were very friendly, I knew they would ask about my life, so I decided to go to other firms. But when I enquired at Fattorini's, I was told they wanted only girls to learn. I knew they didn't want to pay the wages I asked for. I called at Fray's in Tenby Street. Same answer. I was beginning to get depressed when I tried my last call at Butler's in Victoria Street. The money was twice what the other firms wanted to pay, and when I told the foreman that I knew all the processes of the trade I was given a trial to start the next morning. Things seemed to go well, and I felt very happy.

As I walked down Branston Street I smelt fish and chips. I looked in my purse, which now contained only 3s. 3d., which had to last until I could pick up my first week's wages. I bought three pennyworth of chips and ate them from the paper as I walked towards my digs.

As soon as I got there and lifted the knocker, I could smell something nice cooking. When Ellen opened the door to let me in, I made straight for the kitchen and squatted down on the sofa. As I clutched my paper carrier, I heard her say, 'Are you all right? You look very pale.'

'I'm just tired, Ellen. I've been walking about all day lookin' for work. Now I've found what I want – I'm to start tomorrow mornin' at eight o'clock.'

'I'm so pleased for you, and I must get another key cut for you, Kate. Now if you will put your things upstairs and have a wash, I'd like you to sit down with me and have a bit of supper.'

'Oh thank you, Ellen. I 'aven't 'ad time really to buy meself anything, only a few chips,' I said.

I couldn't tell her I had only a few coppers in my purse after buying the clothes.

I took the carrier bag up to my room and put it in the wardrobe with my coat. I washed my face and hands in the washbowl, and after combing my hair (which was losing its waves) I hurried downstairs. Ellen was already serving the stewed meat and vegetables in the dishes on the table, and as we both sat down to eat I felt very awkward when she bent her head and closed her eyes to say grace. I did likewise.

Each time I took a mouthful I thought about my children, wondering if they were happy and having good meals. I hoped too that they were not missing me as much as I was missing them. 'It won't be long', I said to myself, 'before I pay them a visit, and later when I find a real home I shall bring them back where I can love and care for them.'

I started my new job and worked hard for many long hours, yet I was turned down when I asked for a rise. I was dissatisfied, knowing I was worth more than two pounds a week. A few weeks later I heard that Mr Butler had too many orders to cope with and was advertising for outworkers. As soon as I asked about this, he refused, but when I asked for my cards he changed his mind. With all the knowledge I had stored away in my memory, I knew I could run my own business.

I was now feeling ambitious. During that Easter week I found an empty dilapidated top-floor room which I was able to rent for 12s. 6d. a week. But first I had to buy the tools of the trade. I knew firms had tools on approval, but I hadn't enough money to start. I had big ideas and wanted to be independent and have young girls working for *me*. I prayed that I could make it a success. So with hard work, scrubbing and cleaning those old wooden benches and several three-legged stools, I started my trials, but little did I think how many hurdles I would have to jump before landing on my feet in success.

I knew where to buy all the tools and enamels I needed, but I didn't have money in the bank. I couldn't ask there. So I took a chance. Sink or swim. I began to push my luck. I went to see Harry Smith, who owned the ironmonger's shop on the corner of Hockley Street and Key Hill. When I explained to him what I was going to do, and what tools I needed, he said I could have them on a weekly basis and he would send one of his workmen to deliver. But I had to have a guarantor, my landlord of the premises at 90 Spencer Street, Hockley.

The tools came two days later. That same afternoon I tried my luck at Hutton's in Great Hampton Street, who already supplied enamels to different firms. They were pleased to hear I was starting out on my own, and said I could hold an account (whatever that was – it was all double Dutch to me). But I signed the paper and had some enamels on approval.

Now I was halfway there. I had Carborundum files, iron panning, a mortar and pestle to grind the enamel down (today it is sold in powder form), a pair of old patched foot-bellows and a blowlamp. For the first two weeks, when the work started to come in, I sat for many hours at the workbench alone, and felt very lonely. I was receiving more work than I could cope with, but I was afraid to refuse the orders in case I lost them altogether – I didn't want to be a flop. Later I put a notice on the wall outside asking for young girls to learn the trade and a cleaning woman, also a pumice polisher. A few days later I employed two young sisters and during the following months I had twelve girls working with me at the long bench, side by side.

Now I was prospering, I had to have a car to fetch and take the orders and the heavy crates of motor plates. I bought a little second-hand Austin Seven. My brother Jack taught me to drive, but the first time I took the driving seat the wheels were so narrow I got stuck in some tramlines.

You didn't need a driving test, neither did I have a licence. When the Whitsun holiday came I closed my small business for a few days and drove off to see the Matron at the Homes. It was then that I got a shock: I was told my children had been moved to Dr Barnardo's Homes in Barkingside, and if I wished to see them I was to go there – where another disappointment awaited me.

# Dr Barnardo's

I had made up my mind now that whatever happened I was determined to visit my children on the following Sunday.

On Saturday morning I went to the market and bought a basket of fresh fruit, and during the afternoon I made a large fruit cake to take the next day. Later that evening, my brother Jack called to ask me to lend him the car.

'I'm sorry, Jack, but I need it meself to go to visit the children in the Homes.'

'But yer carn't drive all that way on yer own!'

'Well, I had thought of asking you to drive me down.'

As soon as I saw him hesitate, I said, 'Well, if you can't manage to come, I'll go on me own.'

'But it's miles away! You'd never manage to drive all them many miles!'

'Well, I've made up me mind, even if I have ter push it!'

'No need ter lose yer temper. But if I can borrow the car for tonight, I'll bring it round early tomorra an' I'll promise yer ter tek yer. What time yer thinkin' of leavin'?'

'About seven o'clock in the morning.'

'Very well, be ready, I'll fill 'er up with petrol an' we'll tek it in turns to drive.'

'Thanks Jack, I'll be ready,' I replied.

I was pleased he'd be coming with me, as I wouldn't have known what to do if the car broke down.

Although my brother had given me driving lessons, I had never taken that old Austin Seven anywhere out of the district, yet I had plenty of confidence to drive her anywhere.

On Sunday morning I was up early, had my breakfast and got dressed ready. Six o'clock came. I kept gazing up at the alarm clock, waiting for it to point to seven. Yet that hour seemed like an eternity. As soon as the alarm went, I sat

down and waited for Jack to walk in. Quarter-past seven.
Then half-past seven. But still he hadn't arrived. I began to
wonder if he would keep his promise, or if the old jalopy had
broken down? I was thinking how foolish I had been to trust
him. I was almost in tears when I heard the car come rattling
along the cobbles and pull up outside.

As soon as I rushed outside and saw him at the wheel I
yelled, 'Where've yer been? I've been waitin'! Since seven
o'clock!'

'Sorry, Sis, I overslept. Any'ow, jump in if yer ready.'

I fetched the fruit and the cake and a bag of boiled sweets,
put them in the back seat and sat beside my brother, who
stopped to light his Woodbine, then we were off.

How well I remember how that old car went! After a few
miles of rattles and shakes, Jack said it was time for me to
take the wheel and give him a break. But I was enjoying
sitting back and didn't want to drive, so I made the excuse
that I felt safer if he drove.

'Why are yer afraid ter drive now, when I taught yer all
yer wanted ter know?' he snapped.

'But Jack, that was only around the district, not all the rest
of the miles we've got ter go.'

'Well, we'll take it in turns,' he replied. 'Get out.'

We changed over and I took the wheel, after he had given
me directions. As I drove past Banbury, Jack told me not to
do more than thirty on the clock. 'Otherwise the bloody
thing will fall to pieces!' he cried.

I took it steady for a while, between twenty-five and thirty,
then I saw that my brother was nodding off.

I thought it was a pity to wake him – anyway, by now I
was enjoying driving, with little traffic on the roads apart
from a few horses and carts. But after a while I too was
getting tired, and I hit the kerb. Suddenly the car shook. Jack
woke up with a start, grabbed the wheel and steered it into
the tram tracks. Those wheels and tyres were so narrow and
well-worn, we got stuck in the tramlines. I saw a tram
approaching, got scared and jumped out. Several people on
their way to church were staring at us.

'Get back in there!' Jack shouted, 'an' steer while I push the bloody thing!'

I tried and tried but the old thing wouldn't budge, and when I looked behind and saw the tram coming I began to get scared and jumped out again and stood on the pavement holding my breath. What if that tram driver couldn't stop? I thought. Jack could be killed.

But I was relieved when I saw him put his arms up in the air to wave the driver to stop a few feet away. When the conductor came to see what the trouble was, he began to smile. 'Well I never,' I heard him say. 'Where do you think yer gooin' in that ol' boneshaker?'

'It's a long story, mate,' Jack replied, 'but if you'll 'elp me ter get it out of the tramlines we'll be on our way.'

Jack called me back into the driving seat, and as he and the conductor pushed from behind we got out on to the road again, and as the tram passed us the driver and conductor smiled and waved.

I was glad when Jack said he would drive the rest of the way.

After stopping at little tea shops for cups of tea and a bite to eat, and to cool the engine down, we arrived at Dr Barnardo's Homes in Barkingside at about two o'clock.

Seeing the big wrought-iron gates wide open, Jack drove straight in. The outside of that grey stone building was like the outside of a prison. As my brother parked between two large cars, I thought my old boneshaker looked like something from Noah's Ark. Yet it had served its purpose.

As we approached that tall, grey, dismal-looking stone building, we saw an elderly woman dressed in a shabby, faded grey frock. Later I was to find out she was one of the Homes' helpers, who were called Mothers.

She looked very nervous and when she asked who we were, I told her I had come to see my children. 'But this is Sunday, I'm afraid they won't let you see anybody on a Sunday,' she said, rather sadly.

'But I've come a long way – from Birmingham – and I must see my children!'

'I'm so sorry, dear, if it was left to me I'd take you, but then I should get into more trouble than I'm in now. But you can try knocking on the door.'

As she walked hurriedly away she called out, 'I wish you luck, dear.'

As soon as she was out of sight, my brother remarked how scared she looked. 'P'raps she's one of the inmates,' he added. 'Anyway, come on, Kate, let's knock and ask.'

I lifted that iron knocker and dropped it on the big oak door for all I was worth. I heard its echo, but no one came, until Jack made two more attempts. We heard the bolts being drawn back and the door opened. We were faced with a very large, buxom, severe-looking Matron in a long grey dress and a stiff white starched pinafore, a white bonnet tied beneath her double chin. She cried, 'What do you want? Go away!'

When I told her who I was and why I had come, she replied, 'There's no business done on Sundays, you call on Saturdays between two and four o'clock!'

She was about to close the door on us when my brother explained the miles we had travelled to see my children and that we weren't going until we got some kind of satisfaction.

'Well, you'd better both step inside while I make some enquiries.'

I shall never forget that large, cold, dismal-looking room with its dark-green-painted brick walls. All it contained was one oak high-back chair and a large oak writing-desk with inkwells and pens and several ledgers. In the opposite corner of the room was another oak door.

Everywhere seemed so quiet – not a sound or sign of either adults or children.

When the Matron had asked my name and address and the names of my children, she began to open up the ledger. It was then that I was told my son John had been transferred to Watts Naval Training School, and that Jean and Mary were soon to be fostered out to King's Lynn, Norfolk. Kathleen, being the eldest, would be staying.

'But can I see my children now, if only for a few minutes, *please*?' I begged.

But when that hard-faced Matron said 'No visiting on Sundays!' I broke down and wept.

'Please, please,' I pleaded again. 'I must see them, I've come such a long way!'

'Those are the rules!' she replied sharply. 'Have you a pass?' she added.

When I shook my head she said, 'Well, you'll have to wait here while I get you one. Then you can visit on Saturdays only, two till four.'

'But what about my nephew John?' asked my brother.

'That is another matter. You will have to get in touch with the Training School.'

She went through the other door, and we heard her turn the key behind her. As soon as she'd gone, I sat down on the chair and wept.

'Never mind, Sis, it won't be long before next Saturday, we'll see 'em then,' comforted Jack.

'P'raps she'll change her mind, Jack, and let me see 'em, even if it's only for a few minutes,' I replied.

'I can't see that bloody old battleaxe bendin' even a little!' he growled.

I was still hoping, but she came through that door with only the pass in her hand.

'Take this,' she told me, 'and remember: without it you will *not* be admitted!'

As I handed her the fruit cake and sweets to give to my children, I remember her saying, 'I will see that they receive them. Good day.'

(Years later they told me they never did receive them.)

Suddenly Jack glared up at her and cried, 'It's a bloody pity yo ain't got a few of yer own kids 'ere!'

'We don't ask them to come!' snapped the Matron as she slammed the door against us.

My brother drove us all the way home. I sat in the back seat and cried myself to sleep.

\* \* \*

That next Saturday morning couldn't come quickly enough, but when it did Jack came to say he was sorry, but his boss wanted him to work over to move some machinery.

It was then that my sister Liza and I decided we'd travel by train. We arranged between us that if I should happen to see one of my children I would get them to come along with me through the gates, away to the railway station and on to the train. As soon as we arrived, I happened to see one of the Mothers in the grounds carrying my youngest child. As I tried to grab her, she screamed. The next thing I knew, my pass was taken from me and I was ordered off the premises.

Although I made several attempts later, I never saw my children again for the next eight years. Although I wrote to them, I never got any reply to my letters, and it was not until they came home that they told me they never received any presents or letters.

During those years from 1931 to 1939 I worked hard day and night saving every penny I could spare to put into the bank to buy a house for my children to come home to.

# The Vicar

When I first applied for outwork enamelling, some firms actually laughed at me. They had never heard of a young woman wanting to start up a business on her own, enamelling badges and motor plates. But my twelve employees and I worked together side by side. The large motor plates I did myself. I would also fetch and carry back the finished work.

One day, as I was carrying a large heavy crate of badges, I happened to meet my brother Frank. As he helped me, he remarked how pale and thin I'd become.

'I'm all right, Frank,' I replied. 'But I can't afford a man's wages yet.'

'Well, let me know if yer want any 'elp, an' don't work so hard or you'll be killin' yerself. The trouble with you is you're feeling too independent,' he added.

'Frank,' I replied as I smiled at him, 'hard work will never kill me. Anyway, I'm thriving on hard work and determination.'

When he carried the crate up the stairs and dropped it on the floor, all the girls looked up at him and smiled.

Before he went he turned and said, 'I wouldn't mind bein' in charge of these pretty wenches.'

Frank was a nice-looking chap in a rugged kind of way. He would have looked handsome if he'd had the right kind of clothes to wear.

I have never forgotten my brother's kindness.

One Easter holiday he came and whitewashed the shop. When I offered to pay he said, 'Just buy me a few fags, I'll be satisfied.' But later I did other kindnesses for him and his wife, for I could never repay them for all the help they gave me during those years of struggle.

Seeing my brother Frank more often, and working at the

bench besides my workers, I didn't feel so depressed. Night-time was worst, when I closed the business and went home to a lonely house. It was then that I would think of my children and wonder if they were happy and well fed.

They had been away from me for over three years now. I hadn't seen or heard from them. So I decided to write again to the Matron of the Homes and tell her I had a well-furnished home and a business. I was now in a position to care for them. I also bought a new car.

Several weeks went by – still no reply.

When I told my brother, he said, 'Why don't you go and see the vicar – p'raps 'e can 'elp.'

'But I don't go to church, Frank,' I replied.

'That won't mek any difference – any'ow 'e knows you and our family. There ain't much 'e don't know,' he added.

'Frank, if he asks me to pray I shall walk away.'

'But why?'

'Because I don't believe there's a God above! I've prayed and prayed too many times and He's never answered *my* prayers!'

'But Kate, God moves in very mysterious ways and . . .'

'Don't start preaching to me, Frank!' I replied bitterly. 'He's never give *me* any signs of help!'

'Well, will you go if I go with yer?'

'I'll have to think about it.'

A few weeks later I thought it over, then one afternoon while there was no service on Frank and I went to see the vicar at St Paul's Church.

The churchwarden asked us our business, and when I told him he told us to take a seat and the vicar would see us.

While we were waiting, I whispered, 'Frank, what shall I say?'

'Just tell 'im the truth about 'ow the Homes are ignoring your letters and could he help. An' stop fidgetin', he won't eat yer.'

As soon as I saw the vicar I began to get nervous. He greeted us and asked why we wanted to see him. I began to stammer, and I was glad Frankie did most of the talking.

Every minute I thought the vicar was going to ask us to kneel and pray, but he didn't, and when he took us into the vestry he said he knew my children were in the Homes. He asked why I had allowed them to go, and I replied, 'It's a long story, Vicar; I feel I cannot explain all the details now, but I was wondering if you could help me to get my children back.'

'Did you sign any forms to consent to them being taken into care?'

'No, Vicar, I took them to Moseley Village Homes for a few weeks, on the understanding that I should have them back when I got a proper home for them, and when I went back there a few weeks later I was told they'd been transferred to Barkingside Homes. Now I've had my pass taken away I can't see them, and they won't even answer my letters or let the children write to me.'

'I don't think there's much I can do, my dear. But I will write to them and see what can be done. You say you are now in a position to have them home?'

'Yes,' I replied.

As soon as I told him about the house I'd bought and my business, he wrote it all down and said he'd do what he could. In the meantime he would get in touch with me. As we came out of the vestry, I was scared in case he asked me to kneel and pray. But he just wished us both good day. As I stopped to put two half-crowns in the box, I saw him whispering to my brother.

As soon as we were outside the church, I asked Frank what he had said to him.

'He said he would pray for you and I was to try to get you to come to some of the services.'

'I'm sorry, Frank,' I replied. 'I don't wish to be a hypocrite, but I see enough of them people as do go pulling people to pieces with their gossip as soon as they leave the church.'

'I know, Kate. But they ain't all bad,' he replied.

'Maybe they're not, but I don't have to go to church. *I* know what's right and what's wrong.'

'Will you go if he has some good news for you later?'

'I'll think about it, Frank.'

As my brother put his arm round my shoulders, my eyes filled with tears.

'OK,' he replied. 'I know what yer mean and how yer feelin'.'

'I hope yer don't think I'm wicked, Frank, just because I don't go to church. But inside that place depresses me. Even when my children were all christened there, and the services I had to hear when my young son was killed and my dad died and my husband died all in the space of four years. Even weddings make me weep, and now I've got this dreadful feeling that my children will be shipped away to Canada or Australia, and I shall never see them again.'

'Yer mustn't think like that, Sis! Them places are only for orphans, or children whose parents don't want 'em. Anyway, they'll have to consult *you* first.'

'Consult *me*! Consult *me*!' I flared up at him. 'They dain't consult me when they removed them from Moseley Village!'

'Well, Kate, let's wait and see if the vicar can help, and in the meantime I'll have half a day off work next Saturday and we'll go and see this Matron you've mentioned.'

After thinking over what he said, I agreed.

I said I was sorry I'd flared up at him. He reminded me so much of our dad, who was also very placid and understanding. Many times during my grief I wished he were still here to give me advice.

My brother came to see me the following Saturday morning, and as promised we caught the early train. But as bad luck would have it, the train was two hours late.

When we arrived at the Homes, we saw parents and relatives just leaving.

'We're too late again, Frank,' I cried. 'What am I going to do?'

'Well, we can't go back now, we're here, so come on, we'll try and see this Matron.'

We hurried along the gravel path and when we knocked on the door, the same strong-faced Matron opened it and stood staring down at us. As soon as I told her I was sorry we were late visiting my children, and the reason why, she replied very severely, 'Rules are rules, not to be broken.'

'But I've come a long way, it isn't my fault the train was late. Please let me just see them,' I pleaded.

'You'll have to come next visiting day!' she snapped.

But when I lost my temper and tried to push my way past her, she called to two of the gardeners to put us outside the gates.

'Come on, Sis, I can see we shall get nowhere here, we'll wait until our vicar gets in touch.'

As we were roughly escorted outside those large rusty wrought-iron gates, Frank called the Matron a fat old cow. But that didn't help any.

Our last resort now was to leave it to our vicar, hoping his influence could help.

The following Sunday evening I stood in St Paul's churchyard and waited until all the congregation had left. As soon as I was sure no one would see me, I entered the church. It was very dark inside; only the odd light bulb lit up the altar. I was somewhat relieved that neither the churchwarden nor the vicar was anywhere in sight, and I had a queer feeling inside me. But now I had got this far, I made up my mind not to go back out without a prayer. I knelt down in front of the altar, and prayed quietly to myself to ask God to watch over my children and to bring news soon from them, also from our vicar.

As I walked slowly outside, I felt better for praying. Some people might wonder why I never attended the church services and sat among the congregation, but everyone knew me around the district and if some of our neighbours saw me they would begin their gossiping again. That's one thing I couldn't stand, nor being stared at.

But I went alone three nights running. Only the warden and the cleaner ever saw me as I knelt to pray.

Then one evening the vicar called to tell me he had spoken to the Matron, and I would be having a visitor in a few days' time.

When I asked him if he had seen my children, he said he had and that they were happy and well taken care of. I plied him with all sorts of questions, but he seemed reluctant to say any more, only that I would hear more when my visitors called. And I was to have patience and pray.

Several weeks passed, but still no one came, so I lost faith in going to church to pray. As soon as I told my brother Frank the news, he said, 'You must have patience, Sis.'

'Patience! Patience!' I cried. 'I've even been to church and tried to pray, but God ain't answered my pleadings. It all seems to me a waste of time. If only He would give me some sort of sign, I'd be satisfied. I think I'd do better going to the chapel and asking Father O'Brien if he'll help,' I added.

'How do yer think he can help? He's a Catholic priest. I don't think he'd even listen to yer, and if he did he'd have yer in his confessional box to rake up all yer past.'

'But I've got nothing to hide or be ashamed of, Frank. If parting with my children was a sin, then God help me.'

'Well, Kate, be advised by me: *don't* go to that Catholic priest, you'll only get more upset, so just wait a bit longer until you hear from the vicar again. Now let's have a cuppa tea.'

While we sat drinking our tea, he began to change the subject by talking about when we were young children and begged orange-boxes for our makeshift bed and a bug-infested flock mattress to lie on.

'And you remember the factories where we used to stand with bare feet and in rags, begging for food?' he added.

'Yes, Frank, I remember those days all too well.'

Just as he was about to carry on talking, I heard a knock on the door. My brother answered – there stood an elderly man and a middle-aged woman, both with briefcases under their arms.

I guessed at once who they were when the man asked if I was Mrs Flood.

'Yes,' I replied. 'Will you come in?' I added, as I saw nosy neighbours staring across the street.

'I'll be off now, Kate,' Frank said. 'I'll see you later.' As he kissed my cheek and said 'ta-ra', the woman stared at us both and asked who he was.

'He's my brother,' I replied sharply. I wondered who she thought he was.

'We have come from the Homes about your children and details of your circumstances. We would like to look around the house.'

'You also have a business?' the man asked.

'Yes,' I answered as I began to show them round my home.

The two inquisitors looked around every room – they even turned the bedclothes down from the beds I had kept well aired ready for when my children came back.

After saying they were satisfied that everything seemed in order, they asked to see my small business.

I sat in their car (different from my old boneshaker I had to get rid of) and after looking around and taking notes, they told me they were satisfied and would send in their reports, and I should have my children back in due course.

But although I waited anxiously for two more long years, it wasn't until 1939 that my children came home to me. And then the war had started.

# My Daughter Jean

While my children were at Dr Barnardo's, Mary and Jean were transferred to live in the country: King's Lynn, Norfolk. But my daughter Kathleen, being the eldest, was kept at the Homes to do heavy chores. One of their punishments was that if they didn't eat what was put before them it was served up at the next meal, and the next, until they were so hungry they were glad to eat it. Sometimes cold mutton set hard on the plate. Jean also told me that she had cake once a week, when a visitor called, but she didn't like caraway-seed cake and wouldn't eat it. For her tea the following Sunday she had to sit down to a plate of caraway seeds, which she was forced to eat in front of all the other children.

When I brought my daughters back home they were no longer the babies I almost lost, but young girls. They had no understanding of the world outside the Homes. I had to try to make them understand that I was their real mother, yet it was hard for me to explain why I had parted with them. I was determined to give them the love and affection they had missed, but I found it hard to understand their ways at times, and they mine.

Soon after I had enrolled my youngest daughter Mary at the school in Soho Road, she was evacuated with the other children and their teachers to Wales. I didn't want to lose her again, but I thought it would be best for her to be away from the bombing.

I tried not to let her see my tears as I stood watching her standing with other children on the railway platform, holding her small attaché case and clutching her teddy bear, and with her name on a card and her gas mask tied round her neck. I felt very sad. I was only just getting used to her ways, and now I was parting with her again. But we visited her several

times, and I was pleased to see she was qui[
other evacuees.

Yet I didn't know Jean was missing her si[
began to rebel and cried often. She too coul[
why I had brought her home from the country ˯˯ ˯
Birmingham, full of noise, bombing and sleeping down in air-
raid shelters. Often she used to say she was going to run
away, yet I couldn't keep my eye on her all the time. I had
my business to run.

After a few tantrums, she asked if she could go to work
and learn enamelling with her eldest sister. Everything went
smoothly for a while, until Kath became very bossy. They
began their little squabbles.

I knew I was giving more attention to Jean, in case she
decided to run away. Kath became jealous, and the two of
them never could see eye to eye. Often Kath carried tales to
me. At times, I foolishly believed her.

But my three daughters were never angels. Although they
brought me no disgrace, they had their faults, like all teenagers, and many times I used to get exasperated.

On VE Day, 1945, everybody in the streets for miles
around began celebrating, singing and dancing.

Jean and my sister-in-law, who was living with me at the
time, were working for me in my enamelling business in
Spencer Street, which is still in the Jewellery Quarter. As
usual, I left early to go home and get their teas ready, but
they were late coming home, and I began to get worried.

It was two hours later when I saw Jean stumble into the
room, looking very pale. My sister-in-law was trying to hold
her up. I cried, 'Jean! Whatever's the matter?'

'I wanta be sick,' she managed to say as she put her hand
to her mouth.

As I reached for a bowl, Nellie replied, 'She'll be all right,
I'll take her up to bed.'

'No you won't! Help me to lift her on to the settee, while
I run for the doctor.'

Dr Arthur, our family doctor, had his practice in a small
old house in Soho Road.

As soon as he had examined her, he began to stare hard at me. 'How old is this child?' he snapped.

When I told him she was nearly sixteen, he began to bawl out at me: 'Nearly sixteen! You should be ashamed to let her get into this state! This child is drunk! Give her a good drink of salt water, that's all she needs!' and he stormed out.

When I asked Nellie how Jean had got into this state, she replied, 'We all heard it was VE Day over the wireless, so we all downed tools and went across to the Jeweller's Arms to celebrate.'

Next day, when I made enquiries, I was told that my sister-in-law and Jean had drunk a bottle of whisky between them, and were later seen banging on dustbin lids and singing.

Jean was ill for days, but she had learnt her lesson. She never drank alcohol again. Yet my worries were renewed when she began to smoke. However, I was no good example: I too smoked during those war years, but I noticed she never inhaled the smoke.

Today she is a wonderful caring daughter with a loving husband, four lovely daughters, and grandchildren.

I often recall the day when Mary was evacuated with hundreds of other young schoolchildren. I felt very sad about parting with her again, yet as the train began to move out of the station and I waved goodbye, she began to smile as she too waved from the open window. 'Goodbye, Mum,' she called. 'See you and Jean when the war's over.'

'Yes!' I shouted loudly. 'We'll come and visit you soon.'

As I sat on the platform bench, wiping my eyes, I overheard two women beside me talking to each other. Thinking they knew this place where the children were going, I stopped to listen, and I heard one of them say, 'I don't think our lads or us women are goona stand them Germans invadin' England, Betty.'

'Well, I'm glad my three kids will be safer evacuated in the country, Sarah.'

''Vacuated, my foot! I don't know wot yer wanta send the

little buggers away for, it looks ter me as if some of 'em wanta get rid of 'em,' the other woman replied. 'Any'ow,' she added, 'we never sent our kids away in the last war, an' we 'ad the Zeppelins then, like great big floatin' sausages in the air. An' one dropped a bomb on Kynocks.'

'Yes, we know,' replied Sarah. 'But it warn't the same in the 1914 war, everything was different. Now we've got big guns an' aeroplanes, airmen, a navy, and an army.'

'Some bloody army! Them lads won't stand a chance. I remember my two sons had ter train in the streets like thousands of others, up and down the country, with wooden rifles slung over their shoulders, because we 'adn't enough guns!'

'It's no good yer dwellin' on that, them days are gone. An' now we've got more modern equipment *and* we're getting more every day. Any'ow, we've all got to put our shoulders to the wheel, old and young alike, an' 'elp in the war effort.'

'I still think yer should 'ave kept yer children with yer, yer don't know wot they'll be gettin' up to in the country, an' God knows wot'll 'appen to 'em if *we* get invaded.'

'You always look on the black side. Good job we ain't all like you. Any'ow, 'ow's yower Benny, 'ave yer 'eard from 'im yet?'

'No, not yet, 'e ain't bin away long enough ter write, but 'e will. Any'ow, I 'ope Benny wears them warm socks and underpants I've knitted 'im, he feels the cold night air summat awful.'

'Knowin' yower Benny, it won't be long befower 'e finds 'imself a nice little WAAF ter keep 'im warm at nights. Yo and yower Benny! Yer mek me sick. It looks ter me as if yer wanta think about yer old man a bit mower! Any'ow, I can't sit 'ere all day listenin' about yower Benny. Anybody would think 'e was the only pebble on the beach!'

I could see they were both losing their tempers, so I got up and walked away. When I looked back, they were still going at each other.

As soon as I was indoors, Jean asked if Mary had got off all right.

'Yes,' I replied as tears filled my eyes. 'But I still wonder if I've done the right thing, Jeannie.'

'She'll be all right, Mum. Mary's used to living in the country. She'll love it. And we'll go and visit her when she's settled in. Now sit down while I put the kettle on, and we'll have a nice cup of tea.'

# *Phoebe*

During 1940 young men of all ages were no longer seen queuing for their dole money or miserable hand-outs from parish relief. Nor did you see barrow boys from that once-famous Bull Ring, shouting their wares along the side of the open fish market. But to keep up their tradition, old men who had fought in the 1914 war took over their places – their mothers and wives too.

Many families looked forward to a Saturday night out in the Bull Ring, bargaining around the barrows before going into the overcrowded pubs to have a few drinks and talk about the war or the young lives that had been lost.

Many a man or boy sent money home to their loved ones, whatever they could spare. But often some would grumble; you'd hear them say, 'What's the use of bloody money when meat an' vegetables an' clothes are rationed?'

Even soap was rationed, yet there was always the black market. But these traders, who were called 'spivs', were often fined or put into prison. I remember one such fellow, who lived in Graham Street, was a conscientious objector – people called him a 'conchie'. He was in Winson Green prison for a while, but never was he in the forces. He used to say he didn't believe in killing humans, and still sold on the black market.

During those war years I saw my mother only about three or four times. She was a very domineering woman – stubborn too. Often we quarrelled over my children and domestic matters, and she would never go down to the shelters. When the sirens sounded she would always go to bed. My friend Phoebe and I collected everyone from our yards and took them down to the air-raid shelter, but we had several false alarms in Birmingham.

Although I had my small enamelling business in Spencer Street, I gave my services many nights. But we were happy to stay at home when there were no sirens or bombs falling. One night I was invited to a party at the Bridge Tavern in Hunters Vale, owned by Gladys and Arthur Glover. I'd had a few drinks and everyone was merry, until we heard the sirens. Thinking about my two eldest daughters, Kath and Jean, whom I'd left in bed, I fled up Soho Road and down Waverhill Road. But in my hurry I'd forgotten to pick up my handbag with my keys in. I banged and banged, and kicked that door, but my daughters never heard me. There was only one thing left to do: I picked up a brick and smashed the window. As soon as I had climbed through, I flew up the stairs, and when I entered the bedroom I saw that my daughters were sleeping peacefully. But I had to get them downstairs. 'Wake up, wake up!' I cried. 'The sirens have gone!' As soon as we got downstairs, the three of us went into the larder, where we always kept a mattress in case of an emergency. I kept awake while my daughters slept on. It seemed hours as we lay there, yet everywhere seemed so quiet. As soon as dawn broke, I went into the street. When I saw the warden, I said, 'I wonder when the all clear is going to sound?'

'All clear, Mrs?' he replied, staring at me as though I was mad. 'The all clear went about eleven o'clock last night.'

What I'd thought was the warning was the all clear! We had many a laugh over that night, and the hours we spent in that cold larder. But it cost me thirty shillings to have that window and frame mended.

I would have loved to join the ARP, but I didn't have the time, working all day. But I spent many nights helping the wardens with fire-watching.

Mr Smith, who owned the glass shop just round the corner from where we lived, was one of the wardens, and beneath his shop was the shelter. I remember he asked me if I'd marry him as soon as the war was over. But although I liked him as a friend, I refused him. I didn't feel I wanted to get married again. Anyway, I had my independence now, and my daughters to think about.

We had all kinds of people down in that shelter – which used to be a storeroom – that ran underneath the front shops. There were men home on leave, women and children – even babies in arms. We even had men and women tramps, whom we would have passed by at any other time, but everybody helped everybody else in those days, whether they were rich, poor or indifferent. I noticed now that my neighbour, Phoebe, spent more time in pubs. One night I asked her why.

'Yo wanta try it, Kate, it 'elps yer ter ferget wot's 'appenin' around yer.'

Although I liked a glass or two of stout, I knew when I'd had enough.

Phoebe was really having trouble with her husband, yet it wasn't for me to pry. So as long as we got along well together, I knew she would tell me all in good time.

Many times we went fire-watching together, putting out incendiaries with sand from bins on the pavement. Phoebe had a sense of humour, and often when we lit a fag she would tell me funny stories about her family life, and how her husband set fire to the bed and what he put it out with. When I said I didn't believe her, she said, 'It's true. But I'll leave yer to guess. We had no water in the 'ouse!' she added.

'He never did!' I cried, laughing.

''E did, Kate, 'e pulls it out an' pisses anywhere, even in the entry, can't even wait till 'e gets up the yard ter the closet.'

I often smiled at the many stories she told me as we patrolled the streets, and one night I asked her about her three young children.

'Have you ever thought of having your children evacuated?'

'No, if we do get bombed I'd like us ter goo all together.'

'But Phoebe, that's bein' selfish.'

'Selfish or not, while they're 'ere, I want 'em where I can see wot they're doin' any'ow. 'Ow's your young Mary doin' in Wales?'

'She's fine. She loves the country and we go to visit when

we can. But I still miss her, Phoebe. I've only had them back from the Homes fifteen months, and I'm still finding it hard to do what's best for them. I love 'em, but sometimes Jeannie rebels.'

'But why? She's such a nice kid.'

'Well, she was brought up in the country with Mary after leaving the Homes, and misses her. And neither of them couldn't understand why I brought them back to Birmingham and the bombing. And Jeannie worries me when she won't go down the air-raid shelter when the sirens start.'

'Where's yer son John, then, can't 'e do summat to 'elp?'

'My John's in the navy – that's where the Homes sent him – and he was only just fifteen and now he's in the midst of it all, and I pray every night to the good Lord to keep him safe. Now come on, Phoebe,' I added, 'it's time we took the cocoa down the shelter before it gets cold – they'll all be waiting.'

That very same night we could hear the thud of the bombs being dropped and the gunfire in the distance. Many of us would pray they wouldn't come nearer. But as they were heard to get louder and louder, almost overhead, old and young alike soon crammed into the shelter. My one thought was my two daughters, whom I'd left in bed. But as I looked among the crowd I was relieved to see them sitting on an empty crate.

Suddenly the lights went out, and as we lit some candles we heard the bombs falling nearer. We could hear fire engines clanging their bells as children began to wake up and scream, while mothers tried to pacify them by singing to them.

All at once, as I stood near one of the bunks, someone nearly toppled over me. When I shone my torch on to the floor, I could see it was an old drunken tramp who had crept in later. She had rolled off the bunk on to the floor still half awake, and with help from Phoebe I picked her up and laid her back on the bunk, where she closed her eyes and began to snore again.

All through that night, until dawn, the Germans were dropping their bombs and incendiaries – anywhere.

Phoebe and I offered to go out to help the warden put out

some smaller fires, but he was adamant. 'You stay where you are!' he cried out. 'You'll be more help trying to calm the children down.'

That night will live in my memory for ever. So will the dawn. One bomb hit Woolworth's, next to the bank. Many fools ran out when they saw slips of paper flying through the air, which they thought were pound notes from the bank; two boys were killed.

As soon as daylight came and the all clear sirens sounded, everyone rushed out to see if their homes were still there, but many had been badly damaged. Kind neighbours took them in. Just as I was leaving with my two daughters, the warden came towards me.

'I'm sorry to tell you this, Mrs Flood, but I think you had better try and make your way down Camden Drive. It's had a direct hit.'

That was in April 1941 – my mother and sister Mary were killed, with many neighbours and friends.

I shall never forget the day of the funerals. There wasn't a dry eye in the Lane, and as we entered the cemetery I saw men and women alike still digging to make room for those communal graves.

As I stood there and wept, with my brothers and sister Liza, I thought only of the harsh words my mother and I had often exchanged. And the saddest thing of all: it's too late to withdraw them – but they still live in my memory.

If only my mother had come to live with me when I pleaded with her to leave Camden Drive! She wouldn't have been lying there in that communal grave with my sister Mary and the many neighbours on that fatal night in April 1941.

Phoebe, too, was at that same graveside weeping with many other people who had lost loved ones, for she had lost a young brother and her dad, whilst fire-watching.

After that terrible night of bombing there was a lull, and I saw less and less of Phoebe. The only times she came was when she wanted to borrow.

As everything was now on ration it was hard for everyone

to manage. Queuing up for hours outside different shops, you would be lucky if you got three sausages. Other times, after waiting, when it was at last your turn, as soon as you got to the door, you'd see the butcher put a notice in the window: 'Sorry. Try again tomorrow.'

It was on a morning like this that I saw Phoebe at the end of the queue.

'He's sold out, Phoebe, let's try some of the other shops – we might be lucky for a few scrag ends,' I said.

''E ain't sold out! I know 'im, the crafty ol' bleeda! 'E keeps 'is best pieces under the counter, ter sell on the black market. Somebody oughta shop 'im!' Phoebe shouted for all to hear.

'Why don't *you* shop 'im?' cried one of our neighbours, who already had her three sausages.

'You shut yer gob, you ol' bag!' yelled Phoebe. 'I see you've got yower three sausages, an' it's not only sausages 'e lets yer 'ave. It's p'raps a feel of *'is* sausage, if I know 'im.'

Everybody began to laugh, and the neighbour, Mrs Reeves, suddenly screeched, 'I'll wrap these bleedin' sausages around yer bleedin' ear'ole, yer saucy bleeda!'

'Goo on then!' Phoebe shouted back. 'I could do with a feed.'

As Mrs Reeves was about to dash across the way, she stopped and seemed to have second thoughts, for she knew Phoebe was a tough customer. As Phoebe stood waiting for her next move, crowds of bystanders were listening, expecting to see a rough-and-tumble.

'Come on, Phoebe,' I said, pulling her coat sleeve. 'Let's go before the coppers come.'

'All right, all right!' she replied angrily. 'But I'll see that butcher closes down. Anyway,' she added, 'I know where I can get a piece of meat, without any trouble.'

'But where?' I asked.

'There's a bloke I know who's got a butcher's shop.'

'Where?' I asked again.

'It's in Aston, near the House that Jack Built.'

'But I can't go now, Phoebe, I've already spent three

wasted hours trying to get three sausages I dain't get, and my daughters will be waiting for their tea.'

'Got summat nice, then?' she asked.

'Well, no, we got to make do with yesterday's leftover mutton, tough as an old horse,' I added.

'I 'ad some 'orse flesh last week off Alf, an' it was better than a piece of steak,' she replied.

'Who's Alf?' I asked.

''E's this friend of mine who's the butcher – now are yer cummin' or not?' she cried impatiently.

'All right, but I'll have to leave a note where I'm going.'

'Whatever yer do, Kate, don't tell 'em where we're gooin', I'm supposed to keep quiet about him.'

'All right, I'll just say "I won't be long".'

Off we hurried. But as soon as the butcher saw me, he asked, 'Who's 'er?'

'She's me friend,' replied Phoebe.

'Is she all right?' I heard him whisper.

'Yes, she won't say anything.'

'All right, me old cock, but where yer bin 'idin' yerself these days?'

'I'll explain later, but can yer manage to let me 'ave a bit of liver an' a few chops?'

'Anything for you, me darling,' I heard him whisper. I saw him pinch her bottom and put his hand up her skirt. She burst out laughing.

I blushed all over, and wished I hadn't come. I was beginning to feel embarrassed.

As soon as he had given her a parcel and we were outside, I said, 'Why did yer let him do that?'

'Do what?' she asked.

'Pinch yer bottom,' I replied. 'And let him put his hand up yer skirt, and what was yer whispering about?' I added.

'Oh, nothing that would be of any interest to you, Kate. Any'ow, there's no 'arm done, 'e's only me cousin.'

I'd heard that one before, and I wasn't as green as she thought I was.

But I was grateful for the liver, and next day we sat down

and enjoyed our fried liver and onions, and no questions asked. Later, Phoebe came to say Alf had had to go in the army. As everything was rationed, it was hard to manage.

I hadn't seen Phoebe for a couple of weeks, then one day I was surprised to see her knock on my door.

'Can I cum in?' she called through the letterbox.

As soon as she came into the front room, I saw that her eyes were all black and blue.

When I asked her how they got that way, she replied, 'It's a long story, I ain't got time ter tell yer now, but could yer let me 'ave a bit of sugar?'

As I didn't take sugar myself, I gave her what was left in the basin. She said she'd return it later, but she never did. Another day it was a bit of lard, or margarine, then I never saw her again until a week later. And as I opened the door to let her in, she flopped down on the chair. I noticed that her eyes were still discoloured. All at once she asked if I could let her have a bit of tea.

'I'm sorry, Phoebe,' I replied, 'but I only have my two ounces a week and you know how far that goes; you'll have to stew the leaves up.'

'I've got no leaves ter stew up now, Arthur teks 'is two ounce an' shares it with 'is mates at work, an' sometimes I can't even find me ration books, 'e even teks the coupons out and changes 'em for Player's Weights, *an'* some of me clothes coupons,' she added.

'But can't you hide the books?' I replied.

''E'd find 'em any'ow, an' if I don't give 'em to 'im, 'e starts beatin' me. But as soon as this bleedin' war is over, I'm goin' ter leave the drunken bastard, an' the kids.'

As soon as I saw the tears, I felt sorry for her.

'Here you are then, yer better have half of what I've got. But that'll have to be the last.' I gave her half what was in the caddy, and as she went to go out she said, 'Kate, could yer lend me ten shillin'?'

'No, I can't! What yer want ten shillings for anyway?'

'Well, I can get a bit of black market off that bloke in Graham Street.'

'I'm sorry, Phoebe, but I don't encourage people in the black market.'

With that she left, but I remember I was glad of a bit of black market when my daughter Kathleen got married later.

Mrs Hickman, who had a fruit and vegetable shop in Hockley Street, supplied everybody, as long as she could see their money. I knew it was wrong, but it was a temptation – you could get a fine or imprisonment or both. Many times I was worried in case I was found out. But many of us didn't care, for we never knew if we would be alive from one day to the next.

Yet often, if I got an orange or a couple of bananas, I'd give them to a neighbour for her hungry baby. And they never asked how I came by them. No doubt they guessed.

Once I gave Phoebe some tomatoes. When she asked me where they came from I replied, 'It's very hush-hush.'

She was the last person to tell, otherwise I could see her going to that shop and making a nuisance of herself.

The next time she called she walked in and as she sat down on the settee, she asked at once, 'Kate, I ain't cum ter borra any of yer rations, but I was wonderin' if yer could lend me yer fox-fur stole? Yer see, I've bin invited to this birthday party.'

'What party's this?' I asked.

'It's a young woman I used ter work with – lives in Nursery Road,' she added.

I'd always had a soft spot for her, for she hadn't many clothes and often I gave her what I could spare and liked to see her wearing them. I hadn't worn my furs for a couple of years. I'd never liked them anyway, they were still in the wardrobe.

As soon as I brought them down and handed them to her, she cried at once, 'They're lovely, Kate. Wanta sell 'em to me?'

'No, Phoebe, but see as you bring them back – remember, I'm only lending them to yer.'

I would willingly have given them to her, but I could see now I was only encouraging her to come borrowing.

Three weeks later she never came, so I decided this was the last time I would believe or trust her. Therefore, I made up my mind to call at her home and fetch them back.

I had never been inside her house, but as I stood outside I noticed that the place didn't look very wholesome. As I stepped over rubbish, broken bricks and slates, and broken windows, some still holding together with sticking plaster from previous bombings, I wondered then if anyone still lived there. But I had to find out. As soon as I knocked on the door it suddenly flew open wide, and there stood Phoebe's husband, a tall, thin, sallow-faced man. At once I noticed several days' growth of grey stubbly hair sprouting from his chin and upper lip, where hung a half-broken fag. The sleeves of his grubby shirt were rolled up to his elbows, his arms were covered in blue and red tattoos. His trousers were greasy and tied round his waist with his braces. And as he stood there in his stockinged feet, staring at me, he shouted, 'Wot do you want? If yer cum ter see Pheeb, she ain't 'ere!'

'But can I come in and wait?' I asked.

'Yo'll 'ave a lung bleedin' wait then! She's left me, an' me kids!' he bawled.

Just then I saw two grubby little girls, about three or four years old, staring at me as they came and stood beside him.

'Lizzie!' he bawled. 'Cum and fetch these kids in!'

But they seemed scared and ran into the room.

'I'm sorry,' I replied. 'I'll call again.'

I was about to go, when he yelled, 'Wot yer cum for any'ow?'

'Could you tell me if she's left my furs here? If so I would like them back,' I replied.

'No, 'er ain't!' he snapped. ''Er's p'raps took 'em with 'er, ration books an' all!' he added. ''An' if yer *do* see 'er, yer can tell 'er from me, I ain't ever 'avin' 'er back!'

I could see I was getting nowhere, and as I went to go he slammed the door in my face.

I didn't bother about the furs now; all I kept thinking about was those two unwashed, neglected children.

A few days later I opened my door to a loud knock. When I opened it, a young woman stood on the step. I noticed she was overdressed, with well-rouged cheeks and painted lips; also her eyebrows had been shaved and pencilled over. Her hair, I could see, she had attempted to dye blonde, with the black roots showing. She wore long dangling red earrings, a long green dress and a short rabbit-skin fur coat (we used to call them bum-freezers). As soon as I asked who she was, she replied, 'I'm Pheeb's sister, an' I've brought yer furs back.'

I couldn't believe she was Phoebe's sister, she hadn't even mentioned she had one. She wasn't anything like her. As she handed the parcel to me she cried as she looked across the yard, 'I see yer got plenty of nosy neighbours.'

I would have invited her in, then I saw Mrs Carter turn her nose up at her as she passed.

'But why couldn't she come herself?' I asked.

'That's 'er bloody business!' she snapped. 'Any'ow,' she added, 'I'm only 'ere ter look after Arthur's kids!'

I took the furs and as I said 'thank you' I closed the door. As soon as she'd gone I peeped through the curtain to see several women across the street whispering together.

She didn't look the type of person to care for children. Yet, I thought, if she *was* telling the truth, then it was none of my business.

Later that same evening I was to find out from neighbours. She was the barmaid from the Globe Tavern, also Arthur's fancy woman.

A couple of days later, when I opened up the parcel, I found that one of the tails was missing. I took the furs upstairs, pushed them into the wardrobe, and forgot about them – until I decided to have a clear-out. Then I saw that moths had decided to have a loan of them. I put them in an old basket for my daughter Jeannie's cat, Sooty.

I never saw or heard what became of my fire-watching friend Phoebe. Nor her family. I knew only that they had moved before their house was bombed.

# Sal

Many kind neighbours would help each other as best they could in the war years, and often we called each other by our Christian names. Except children. No matter how poor, they were always taught their manners by addressing their elders by their surnames or whatever, and it was always 'Yes please' or 'No thank you'. But often you would get the odd cheeky, but harmless ones. They were always disciplined by their parents or schoolteachers.

Mrs Briggs – Sal, as I often called her – was one of my neighbours. She had two daughters, Florrie and Annie, who were in the land army. She also had three sons, who were too young to enlist with their father. Two of them were working on munitions; the youngest lad, Georgie, was nearly six. He was a lovely little lad who often reminded me of my son John.

Early one morning, Sal came knocking on my door. As soon as I opened it she cried, 'Oh, Kate! Kate! I've just 'ad a telegram from the War Office ter tell me me 'usband is missin'. Wot am I gooin' ter tell me lads?'

When I saw the tears streaming down her face, I said, 'You better come in, Sal, and sit down.'

As she flopped down on the sofa, she began to sob into her apron.

'I'll put the kettle on and make you a cuppa, Sal,' was all I could say, for she was sobbing and crying aloud.

'It's little Georgie, 'e'll break 'is little 'eart when 'e knows.'

I didn't know what to say to console her, but I said how sorry I felt.

I knew she liked a drop of whisky. As I handed her the cup of tea I asked if she'd like some, and she nodded. As I poured it into the cup, I told her I couldn't spare much as it was for

106

the wardens when we had a bad night. As she drank it down she was still sobbing. I said, 'Look, Sal, it could be a false alarm, and you might have another telegram to say he's safe. Then you'll have all yer worry for nothing,' I added, trying to console her.

'But I don't know 'ow I'm gooin' ter tell me lads,' she managed to say.

'Well, Sal, if you think it's best, tell your two eldest, but I should spare little Georgie's feelings until later, as you know he's too young to understand. Anyway, Sal, as I say, it could still be a false alarm.'

After finishing her tea, she said, 'Little Georgie's six termorra an' I promised ter mek 'im a cake, an' 'is little friends 'ave bin invited. But now I feel too upset ter even think about it.'

'Try not to worry, Sal. I know it's easy for me to say don't worry, but if I can help in any way, I will. Anyway, *I'll* make him a cake. I ain't got much as regards ingredients, but if I ask one or two of the neighbours, I'm sure they'll help.'

As she thanked me I hoped she would understand what I had been trying to say, for she was still sobbing as she left.

As soon as the door closed, I found a recipe I had cut out of a newspaper – 'How to make a wartime cake'. It read something like this:

6 oz self-raising flour
2 oz margarine, lard, or dripping
2 teaspoons powdered milk
5 saccharin tablets or black treacle
1 large carrot, scraped and diced small

Put in mixing bowl, add half teaspoon of bicarb.
Mix well with one teacup of water.
Grease tin and put in oven mark four and leave
for one hour.

As soon as it was baked I took it from the oven, but I was scared to think what it would taste like. Anyway, it looked nice and brown.

When I called Sal indoors to see it, she remarked how nice it smelt. 'Wot yer mek it with, Kate?' she asked at once.

'Ha,' I replied, smiling. 'It's a secret, but I did manage to scrounge some of the ingredients off the neighbours. There was only one who refused, and I don't have to tell you who that skinny old skinflint was,' I added.

It was a warm, sunny spring day, so we decided to take a couple of kitchen tables out into the yard, and with the help of whatever the neighbours could spare, we set the tables with bread and jam, bread and treacle and bottles of home-made ginger pop. I decorated the cake I'd made with silver paper and six candles I'd found in a drawer, also a small paper Union Jack in the centre, and placed it in the middle of the table.

After we had set the six odd cups for the pop, the six little lads, including Georgie, were seated. We adults stood by to watch them enjoy their so-called feast. But when it came to the cake, I wondered what it would taste like.

I watched Sal cut six pieces, one for each lad, and it was decided we should all sing 'Happy Birthday' to Georgie.

I was pleased to see that the lads were enjoying the cake, but all at once little Freddy Carter threw his across the table. 'I don't like that!' he cried out. 'It's got carrots in!'

Suddenly his mother gave him a hard slap across his face.

'Yo'll bloody well eat it, or I'll ram it down yer throat!' she cried out as she picked it up.

'But I don't like carrots,' he whimpered.

'Yo 'eard wot I sed! Yo'll eat it an' be grateful!' she replied.

I watched his tear-stained face as he tried. But after the first swallow, I was pleased to hear him ask for another slice. The other kids seemed to enjoy it too.

After the feast was over, Mrs Freer decided to bring out the old gramophone, and as she put on a record and turned the handle, we all began to sing to the old cracked record:

> 'Oh yes, we have no bananas,
> We have no bananas today.
> We've got broad beans, and bunions,

Carrots, and onions,
And all kinds of things they say.
But yes, we have no bananas,
We have no bananas today.'

A few days later little Georgie came and thanked me for his birthday cake and asked when was I going to make another.

'I don't know, Georgie. Everything's on ration, and we can't keep asking for food, that's hard to come by.'

'But I can get some carrots off the farm, an' Freddy is six on Sunday. Could you mek 'im one so we can 'ave another party?'

'Is that the lad who said he didn't like it?' I asked.

'Yes, but 'e did after 'e ate it, an' 'e's asked me to ask yer.'

'I'm sorry, Georgie, but I'll give his mum the recipe, then she'll be able to make it. Anyway, when the war's over we'll have a *big* party, and I'll make you a *real* cake with currants and cherries, and it will have real sugar in. Now be off, or you'll be late for Sunday School.'

Now, in 1944, the war had taken a turn for the better. News was coming over the wireless every hour to say how our planes were bombing Germany. But there was still fifteen months before peace would be declared, and food was still on ration well after the war was over.

Everyone made the best of their troubles and losses, and whenever someone lost their home there was always a helping hand ready and willing to take them into *their* home, which resulted in many being overcrowded. But people still had a real sense of humour.

Often you would hear them singing dirty little ditties and slogans about Hitler and his mistress Eva Braun. In pubs or clubs and even inside the factories where they worked, and wherever you walked, you would see posters stuck to ruined walls, even outside munitions factories. Many of the slogans were there for everyone to read. One poster that was stuck on the outside toilet walls read:

> When Hitler couldn't get his Braun,
> He'd use old Goebbels with the horn,
> But often Goebbels cried with shame,
> Even he couldn't stand the strain.

Slogans like this were there for everyone to read and joke about. But if little kids were heard to repeat them, many would get a spanking – which did *some* good, yet never did them any harm.

Since I never saw or heard any news from my fire-watching friend Phoebe, I found more time for talking and listening to my neighbours' gossip. Yet there was quite an assortment who lived in our district. Some I liked, but to those I didn't I would only say good morning or good evening, whatever the time of day, and walk away.

But I missed my friend Phoebe, and several nights on my rounds I used to get very lonely. I wasn't too brave either. When I told Mr Smith, the warden, that I was thinking of giving it up, he said he would ask one of the other women to accompany me. But it so happened nobody wanted the job, without pay. Then one night, as I left the air-raid shelter to go home to make the usual jugs of cocoa for the kids whose mothers were afraid to have them evacuated, someone tapped me on the shoulder. When I turned round I saw it was Sal.

'Kate, would yer like me ter 'elp yer mek the cocoa?'

I was glad of her offer, and as I thanked her she replied, 'Yer know summat, Kate, I think yer very brave ter do that fire-watchin'.'

'Thank you,' I replied. 'I didn't mind doing it when Phoebe was here to help, but I don't feel so brave now on my own, so I'm thinking of giving it up.'

'Well, Kate, now me sons are on night shift p'raps I could cum with yer.'

'But you know it's only voluntary. There's no pay, and I don't have to do it. But it's better than staying down that stuffy air-raid shelter, and you can feel safer in the street.'

'That's if yer lucky, Kate,' she replied.

'Anyhow, when yer time comes, no matter where you are, that's it,' I added.

As soon as we got indoors we put both the kettles on the gas stove. While we were waiting for them to boil, she said, 'Your 'ouse, Kate, it's nice, an' it's tidier than mine. Anyway yer must cum an' 'ave a cuppa with me some time, an' a chat.'

'I'd love that, Sal, but wouldn't your sons mind?' I asked.

'No, they always talk about yer and say 'ow kind you are an' little Georgie thinks an' ses yer lovely. Tells all the kids in the school too about that cake yer med fer 'is birthday.'

As soon as we had made the two large enamel jugs of cocoa and were on our way to the shelter, she said, 'When Ted and Wilf cum 'ome in the mornin', I'm goin' ter tell 'em I'm gooin' fire-watchin' with yer.'

'Thank you, Sal, but if they object I shall understand.'

'They can't stop me! If once I mek me mind up ter do summat, I do it!'

I smiled and thanked her. From then on we became firm friends. As soon as we entered the shelter, the sirens sounded the all clear for the second time. But no one was in a hurry to leave when they saw us with the cocoa; children and parents stayed to finish it.

The following night Sal came to tell me that she'd told her sons, and she was to please herself. 'But I must be in when they cum 'ome fer their breakfast.' Although I was grateful for her offer, I thought about her youngest, who was only six. 'But what about Georgie?' I asked.

'Georgie will be all right down the shelter, Kate, 'e'll be with 'is friend Jimmy an' 'is mum ses she'll keep 'er eye on 'im.'

We enjoyed a drop of whisky and a fag together – when we could get any.

On quieter nights, when my daughters were tucked up in bed, we would go into each other's homes and talk for hours about when we were young, and about our families. The first time I entered Sal's house I noticed how gloomy it was, with its dark wallpaper and sombre paintings. The furniture was old but highly polished; every corner of the room was very clean, but untidy.

As soon as Sal saw me looking around, she cried out, 'It ain't alwis like this, Kate, but me lads are very untidy, it ain't like your place.'

'I quite understand, Sal. You want to see it when my daughters come in – everything's thrown about and they expect yer to hang everything up after them,' I replied.

'It's betta than the place where we used ter live, but one of these days we're gooin' ter move, no more one down and one up,' she said.

'I know how you feel, Sal. I came from the same district before I made a break.'

When I told her where we used to live, she replied, 'Well, I never! An' I alwis thought yer cum from a posh area.'

'No, my mum had thirteen children, and it must have been a blessing that seven of them died of childhood complaints. The rest of us lived in one living-room, one bedroom, and an attic,' I replied, remembering those hardship years.

'My mum 'ad six before she 'ad me, an' I was seven when she told me they all died young. But I'm not ashamed, Kate, ter tell yer 'ow I was dragged up.'

'I'm sorry, Sal, but do yer feel yer want to tell me?'

'Yes, Kate,' she replied. 'I've never told anyone, not even my sons or daughters, and they've never asked.'

So we lit another fag and drank the remaining whisky, then she began to relate her childhood. And as I sat by the fireside facing her, I listened.

# The Facts of Sal's Life

'When me mum an' me dad died of TB, Kate, I was left an orphan, an' I never 'ad any schoolin'. I can't even read or write, an' ever since I can remember them many years ago I was 'ungry, ragged, dirty, 'air lousy, an' after me mum an' dad was buried by the parish, I 'ad nowhere ter turn to, I even walked miles ter find the 'ouse where me Auntie Maggie lived. But when I did find it, she said I 'ad ter goo an' see me dad's sister, Auntie Maud, who lived in the next yard. When I knocked on the door, an' she saw me, she dragged me inside quick, ashamed the neighbours would see me. She 'ad a man lodger, an' when 'e sat there starin' at me, me aunt cried out, "Look wot the cat's dragged in".

'She sheltered me for a while, but I was knocked from pilla ter post; but I was grateful for the leftovers she fed me, also the flock mattress where I slept in the attic. But I 'ad ter slave like a lackey to earn that.

'I was really scared of Maud's lodger. I knew she slept with him some nights, other nights I used to 'ear 'er snorin' in 'er own room. Sometimes I used to see 'im with a lopsided grin on 'is ugly face, watching me every movement. I could even feel 'im undressin' me with them eyes of 'is. One night when me aunt was out, I saw 'is hand begin to unfasten the buttons on 'is flies. I got scared, then all at once 'e cum grinnin' towards me an' pushed me up against the pantry door, an' when 'e pulled me frock up an' I felt 'is hand inside me drawers, I began ter kick an' scream for all I was worth. As soon as 'e let go of me, I bit 'is 'and an' scratched 'is face. Then 'e slapped me across the face an' threatened ter kill me if I told me aunt. But as soon as she came in, I *did* tell 'er, but she wouldn't believe me, an' yer know what she did, Kate? She said I was a brazen trollop, an' that I must 'ave encour-

113

aged 'im. Then she beat me an' said she was sorry she took me in. The next day she took me to an orphanage. Wot an awful place that was! I was deloused an' bathed in 'ot disinfectant, an' me rags were took away an' burnt, an' after they shaved all me 'air off, I stood naked on that cold stone floor until they decided ter bring a pair of old leather boots, a pair of red flannel drawers, an' a dark-grey smock fer me ter wear. Then I was pushed roughly into a room full of other young girls, dressed an' scalped like meself. After we were lined up we was given a stale crust of black treacle and a mug of warm weak tea. Then after we'd eaten, we was led into another room ter pray fer our blessin's.'

'My God!' I replied. 'Some blessings!'

Then she went on to say, 'I didn't mind the punishments that were dished out ter me. It was when several older girls got together an' often called me lousy. I felt so ashamed, an' I was punished fer fightin'.'

'But having a dirty head was nothing to be ashamed of in those days, Sal. I remember many girls and boys who had dirty heads, but even if you was clean you always used to catch them. But *we* had a nurse who came once a week to our school to inspect us and if she found any nits you was sent home with a note, and I had one once.'

'I can't imagine you to 'ave a dirty 'ead, Kate.'

'I sure did,' I replied. 'It happened one day. Once a year girls who were clean were given a party ticket, called Pentlands Royal Robins. I remember my sister had one; when I asked her why I hadn't got one she said I'd better ask me teacher. I said, "But what if she don't give me one?" Then she said I was to start crying an' to make sure to yell loud. When I did, all I got was the bamboo cane, but teacher said she would find one for me later. And that's the first time I knew I had nits, a few days later, when my teacher gave me a note sealed in an envelope. I thought it was a party ticket. I ran all the way home, and as soon as I saw me mum in the brewhouse doing her washing with the other neighbours, I waved the envelope in the air and shouted, "Mum, I've got a party ticket, look!" As soon as she opened the envelope, she went wild. She caught hold of my hair, and dragged me indoors. "Wot have I done now?" I managed to yell out. She said, "Yo've only showed me up in front of the neighbours! Now I'll be the talk of the street!" She said that wasn't me party ticket, it was a note from the nurse to say I got nits, and when she told me to get her the steel toothcomb and I bent over a piece of newspaper, there was the truth. And after painful tuggings, she washed my hair in Derbac Soap. After that, she cut my hair, which looked like two small fat sausages tied with string. So yer see, Sal, everybody gets 'em, some time or other,' I said.

'But when me 'air started ter grow agen, I still 'ad 'em, an' that was when I tried ter run away. That was when I was fifteen, Kate. But before that, there was another girl – many called her "Tin Ribs" because she was so thin; I never knew 'er real name, an' she never used to say. When we 'appened to speak to each other, I used ter call 'er Lizzie, and she seemed pleased enough. She was an orphan too, an' every mornin' we 'ad ter be up at five o'clock cleaning boots, emptyin' slop buckets, while the elders looked over us. We even had to empty the ashes an' black-lead the grates until yer could see yer face in 'em, Kate. I could talk for hours about 'ow cruel the people was in that orphanage.'

'And did yer manage to get away?' I asked.

'Yes, me an' Lizzie planned it together. But she was a nervous girl, an' kept makin' excuses. But eventually, one night, we escaped through the dormitory winda. It was a pitch-black night, an' we'd only gone a few yards, and Lizzie believed in ghosts. She began to scream, an' said she saw one, so she ran back an' left me. I ran on, but it wasn't long before one of the keepers shone 'is torch on me. We were both punished and beaten an' sent ter bed. Next mornin' me an' Lizzie 'ad ter sit an' watch the other inmates eat their porridge. There was none left for us two. Later that night we were given an 'ard crust of bread an' a cuppa warm watered-down tea. A few weeks later, I saw me chance ter run away agen. I didn't tell Lizzie, I was afraid she'd see ghosts agen an' let me down. So then I was on me own.

'It was while I was marching with the other inmates on our way ter chapel. One of the sisters in charge told us to follow on quietly. As I was the last one left behind to enter the chapel, I saw my chance. I slowly tiptoed backwards – lucky for me no one saw me an' I knowed I wouldn't be missed fer the next hour or more. So I 'ad plenty of time ter run.'

'Wasn't you afraid of being caught again, Sal?' I asked.

'Oh yes, but yer couldn't see me arse fer dust, when once I got outside them chapel gates,' she replied, smiling.

We both began to laugh. Sal lit a cigarette, and when I got up from the chair I asked if I should make a pot of tea.

'Yes, Kate, but I ain't finished tellin' the 'alf of it yet.'

I could see she was now eager to tell me the rest of the story. I too was eager to listen.

As soon as we finished our cigarettes and drank our tea, she said, 'Yer sure yer want ter 'ear the rest?'

'Oh yes, Sal,' I replied eagerly.

'Well, where was I?'

'Yer couldn't see yer arse for dust,' I replied, smiling.

'Well, I dain't know 'ow long I'd bin runnin', until I dropped down exhausted an' fell asleep in an 'edge. I don't know 'ow long I slept when I felt somebody shakin' at me with a stick. When I opened me eyes I saw an old ragged woman bent almost double. She was still pokin' the stick in me when she asked who I was an' where I'd cum from. I was too scared ter tell 'er, so I just said I was on me way 'ome an' was lost. But when she stared down at me she said "Yer tellin' lies, now ain't yer!" She must 'ave noticed wot I was wearin'. When I got to me feet, she said, "Yo ain't lorst at all, yo've run away from them theea orphanages, ain't yer!" An' when I pleaded with 'er not ter send me back, she replied, "Why yer poor 'arf-starved little bugger, I wouldn't send a dog ter die in one of them places. I know, I was brought up in one meself. But that was a long time agoo." Well, any'ow, she told me ter follow 'er ter the cottage, an' when we got inside she put some more logs on the fire and made me sit down while she made me a basin of hot broth. An' while she was makin' it in the corner of the room, I glanced around to see that the place was cluttered up with old clothes, an' there was spider webs 'angin' from the ceilin', and even cockroaches an' rats, but it was a shelter an' somewhere ter 'ide. Yer know summat, Kate, I was fifteen an' a 'alf before I ever knew wot kindness was. That dear old woman looked after me, fed me, an' give me a warm straw mattress ter sleep on, an' in return, all I 'ad ter do was keep 'er cottage clean an' do 'er washin' an' cookin'. It dain't tek me lung ter get rid of them spiders, an' them cockroaches an' rats. She was like an old lost lovable granny I'd found.'

'Didn't anyone find out where you were?' I asked.

'No, that tumbledown cottage was miles away from any-where an' everybody. An' yer know wot, she kept me 'idden away till I was seventeen. She 'ad one son who used ter cum ter visit 'er in an old truck. That was only once a month. But 'e brought us vittles an' was kind to me too. But she was very old an' I cried for days after she died. An' when the son came an' said I 'ad ter leave, I got into a terrible state. But when I told 'im I 'ad nowhere ter goo, 'e said I could stay on a bit longer until 'e sorted things out.

'After a while 'e said 'e was comin' ter live there, an' if I would still take over the chores, I could stay. When I put me arms around his neck an' kissed 'im and thanked 'im, 'e just smiled. 'E was ten years older than me. After a while 'e came to live there. 'E was very kind to me, Kate, an' I liked 'im, an' one night we slept together an' med luv, that led ter more luvmekin'. When I got pregnant an' me first babby died only two days old, 'e asked me ter marry 'im. After we married 'e sold that old cottage. That's where we cum to terday, an' where me two daughters an' me three sons were born, an' I don't think anybody 'as gone through the mill like I 'ave.'

'We all have a cross to bear, Sal. I too had a hard life when I was young and suffered too, only under different circum-stances. I wasn't an orphan, but I had a very cruel mother. Maybe, one day, I'll tell you about my family and how hard and cruel my mother was. I hated her at times, Sal. But when we grow older and have a family of our own, it's not until then we realise what our parents have gone through to rear us, or even *try* to, in a back-to-back dilapidated house full of fleas, and bugs, and no money coming into the household. Everybody in the district had sad moments and heartbreaks, but time heals all wounds, and *my* happiest days was when I attended school.'

'If I'd 'ave gone ter school p'raps I would 'ave 'ad a better life,' she replied.

'Anyway, Sal, we got to live for today and our children. We never know what tomorrow will bring while this war's on, and we can't see into the future, otherwise we'd plan our lives to suit ourselves.'

'I suppose yer right, Kate. But I feel better now I've told you. An' yer know summat,' she added, 'you're the first one I've felt like talkin' to. I ain't ever spoke about me life before, not even ter me sons an' daughters.'

'Have they ever asked?'

'No. I'd feel ashamed, an' they already know I can't read or write.'

'You've nothing ter be ashamed of, Sal, but one day, when they get married and have a family of their own, they may ask, or their grandchildren will, so believe me, don't be scared – or ashamed – to tell them. I'm sure they'll understand.'

'I 'ope so,' she replied.

After we had wished each other good night, I called out, 'See yer tomorrow, Sal – that's if we don't hear the sirens wailing.'

We didn't. That was one of the good nights and we enjoyed a welcome night's sleep.

# Florrie Comes Home

Sal had very bad arthritis in her hands, and often when I found time I would help her to do her washing and ironing.

One Saturday morning, as her three sons were sitting down to breakfast, I called and gave the boys their shirts I'd ironed. They were always grateful, and so was I for the kindnesses they did for their mum and me. Fetching coal from the wharf and cleaning our windows – nothing was too much trouble for them. Sal was very proud of her sons. I was about to leave when Ted said, 'Georgie, move off that chair and let Mrs Flood sit down.'

I thanked Georgie and sat down. Sal handed me a cup of tea and Georgie cried, 'Yer cum ter mek me another cake?'

'Not this time, Georgie, but I've promised you the big one when the war's over,' I replied as I smiled at him.

'Yer won't forget then, will yer?' he asked, smiling back.

'Now yo goo out an' play!' his mother told him, 'an' stop yer mitherin'.'

As soon as he'd gone and the two elder boys had finished eating their breakfast, and helped me and their mum to wash and wipe the crocks, they went into the other room to play dominoes, leaving me and their mum to sort over the dirty clothes ready for the brewhouse on Monday morning. And as we were chatting together, the door suddenly flung open and in came Sal's daughter, Florrie.

It seemed only yesterday when she came to me and told me she was joining the forces, away from her drunken bad-tempered father. She was a lovely-looking girl, and very smart she looked in her WAAF uniform.

As soon as her mother saw her, tears fell as she flung her arms about her. And as Florrie picked up Georgie and hugged

119

him, Sal called out, 'Ted, Wilf! Cum an' look who's cum 'ome!'

As soon as they came into the living-room and saw their sister, Wilf cried out, 'I thought it was me dad!'

'That's a nice greeting, I must say!' Florrie replied. 'I thought you'd be over the moon to see me.'

'We are, we are, Sis,' Ted replied excitedly. 'But we 'ad news from the War Office ter say our dad was missin', and we never expected it ter be you.'

'Well, come and give me a kiss, then,' she exclaimed.

While they were embracing, I thought it was about time I left them to enjoy their meeting. But as soon as I said I was going, Florrie replied, 'You don't have to leave, Mrs Flood. I'm pleased to see you, and I wish to thank you for doing what you can for me mum.'

'That's all right, Florrie. It's nothing really, but what are neighbours for – only to help in these wicked times.'

'Mum's never mixed with any neighbour before, and Ted has written to me often telling me how she's took up fire-watching with you.'

'It's quite fun at times – that's when we get a quiet night,' I exclaimed. 'And when we *do* have to go down the shelter it's better than being at a variety show. The different people we meet with their sense of humour,' I added.

'Yer carn't beat the British for that,' Wilf piped up. 'Any'ow, why dain't yer send us word yer was comin'?' he added.

'I suppose your answer would have been "I'd 'ave med yer a cake." Any'ow,' she added, 'I only got forty-eight hours' leave.'

'Well, let's all sit down,' her mum replied, 'an' tell us 'ow yer bin.'

As we all sat, I asked Sal if I should make a pot of tea.

'I was wondering when you was going to make one. Yer know something? I ain't had a decent cuppa since I left here, only canteen bloody swill, and that tasted like maid's water.'

Suddenly little Georgie, who had been standing in the background listening, cried out, 'Maid's water? Wot's that?'

His sister just smiled at him, but felt she couldn't explain. But she opened her bag and pulled out a small bar of chocolate. 'Here you are, Georgie, now go out and play.'

He didn't need telling twice. Off he ran to find his playmate Jimmy.

As soon as the kettle boiled I made a fresh pot of tea, and when Florrie had drunk hers and asked for a second cup, Ted began to tease her. 'I betcha 'ad a good time, Sis, with the men in uniform.'

'If yer call it having a good time, our Ted – you'd be surprised. There's nobody *I* fancied in that camp, they're quite a mixed bunch. There's the tough ones we all call guys since the Yanks came, then there's the comical guys, who only brag about the good times they'd had outside the camp, and then there's the quiet ones, who never make any effort to have a conversation, and most of them are married, and them as wasn't had a heyday with some of the WAAFs, who couldn't refuse them. And many danced with two left feet,' she added.

'Well, any'ow, love,' said her mum, who had been listening quietly, 'we're all glad to see yer safe an' well. Wot about another cuppa, love? Do yer mind mekin' another pot, Kate?'

I didn't mind in the least, for I was eager to hear more.

'We'll tek yer down ter the local, Sis, ternight, and buy yer a drink,' Ted piped up.

'Oh, an' we'll show the lads wot a smashin' looker we've got fer a sister,' Wilf added, smiling and winking at her.

'Go on with yer. I bet yer say that to all the girls you meet,' replied Florrie, smiling across at her brothers. 'Anyway, ain't my brothers started courting yet, Mum?'

'I don't think they bother about anybody yet, love. I suppose they will when the right ones cum along, or p'raps when yer dad cums back from the war. That's if 'e cums at all,' she continued, as the tears filled her eyes.

'What yer mean, Mum, if he comes?' exclaimed Florrie.

But when Sal tried to explain more about the sad news, Florrie didn't seem a bit disturbed to hear that her dad was missing. She only replied, 'He won't be missing long, Mum, if I know him. As soon as the war's over he'll turn up like a bad penny.'

'We've told 'er that, Sis,' both lads replied, for they remembered – and so did I – the sort of life he led Sal and his family before he joined the army.

As soon as Florrie saw her mother's tears, she quickly changed the subject. 'Don't forget to write and let me know when you two start courting,' she said, turning to her brothers and smiling.

'There's nobody around 'ere we fancy,' replied Wilf.

'But yo've forgotton, yer fancy old "Vinegar Tits"!' Ted began to tease.

'What did yer say, Ted?' asked his sister.

'Old Vinegar Tits,' he replied, grinning all over his face.

'And who's she?'

'She's that fat old bag across the yard,' answered Ted.

'Yer wanta keep clear of 'er,' his mother piped up.

Florrie was now all ears. 'And why do yer call her Vinegar Tits?' she asked.

'Well,' Ted replied, as both lads started to smile, 'the other day it was very 'ot, an' everybody sat outside on their doorstep ter get cool, when we saw Fanny Green come out and stood on 'er doorstep an' we noticed she 'ad 'er blouse wide open ter keep 'er tits cool, an' as . . .'

'That's enough of that, Ted! Yer sister don't wanta 'ear any mower about that brazen trollop! Nor 'er daughters,' she added.

'It's all right, Mum,' said Florrie. 'We hear and see a lot more than that where we're stationed – some of the talk and carry-on would make your hair curl. So go on, Ted, you was saying . . .?'

'Well, she was standin' theea where all the neighbours could see, almost showin' 'er belly button, when a wasp, thinkin' it was a nice place to settle, landed on one of her tits. Then, all at once, we saw 'er run down the yard shoutin' "Pull it orf! Pull it orf! Somebody pull it orf!" And when she managed to tear off 'er blouse, and came runnin' terwards me screamin' an' swearin', I dain't know wot ter do fer laughin', an' so was everybody else who saw the performance.'

'Did yer knock it off?' his sister asked, as she too began to smile.

'Not on yer nelly, Sis. Now if it 'ad been a young pretty wench like yourself, we might 'ave,' Wilf replied. 'Anyway, as soon as everybody saw 'er dirty tits 'angin' like shrunken bladders, nobody would tek any notice.'

Suddenly we all began to laugh out loud as Wilf then tried to demonstrate.

'Only Mrs Freer, she came runnin' towards 'er with a bottle of vinegar an' poured it all over 'er tits. And that's why we all calls 'er Vinegar Tits.'

'But what will happen if she hears yer call her that?' Florrie asked.

''Er knows,' her mother replied. 'Yer can call *'er* whatever you'd a mind ter, she's too thick-skinned ter bother.'

'P'raps she's deaf, Mum.'

'Not 'er, she can 'ear when she wants to.'

That evening we all went down to the local pub, The Stores, on Soho Road, for more stories about the men and girls in Florrie's camp.

# Florrie Goes Back

Monday morning came all too soon for Florrie's mum and her three sons. Before Florrie was ready to leave, she came to see me and wish me goodbye.

I'd already made up a small packet of tea and sugar and some biscuits I'd been saving, also a couple of laundered hankies. She was reluctant to take them at first, but I made sure she did, and as she thanked me she said, 'Mrs Flood, I'm pleased my mum has a friend she can talk to – you see, she never has mixed with any of the neighbours much.'

'Well, Florrie, your mum keeps herself much to herself.'

'I know,' she replied. 'But I notice she speaks well of you, and so do me brothers.'

'I think your mum thinks all the neighbours are a bad lot, but they're not all bad, not when you get to know them. Only the one your brothers call Vinegar Tits – she's also got two daughters about your age, an' they're nothing but trouble and their mother ain't any better. All the neighbours steer clear of 'em, they give the place a bad name when they bring the Yanks home, and now one of 'em is in the family way an' believe me, Florrie, it won't be long before the other daughter's the same.'

'But what's their dad do about it all?'

'That weedy little sponger! I don't think he bothers. He can always be seen in the Frightened Horse, with the Yanks buying him booze and fags.'

'I often wonder about our Annie; my brothers say she hasn't written since she moved up to Scotland and joined the Wrens. I know me mum worries over her too. I wish this bloody war was over, then we could all settle down again!' she exclaimed bitterly.

'But what about your dad? Do you think he'll settle down?'

'I hope so, Mrs Flood,' she replied. 'But if he don't, and he begins his old tricks agen, the lads are older now to deal with him, so I hope he'll think twice before he starts his drunken brawls agen. That's if he does come back!' she added bitterly.

'Don't feel too bitterly about him, Florrie – after all, he is your dad and the war years may change him, and many more like him, for the better.'

'I hope so,' she replied. 'It's been nice having you to chat to, and thanks for helping Mum and the lads,' she added.

'Think nothing of it, Florrie. I like your mum and your brothers; I only wish I had three sons like them. But I have only my three young daughters, and my son John is in the navy, on one of the big battleships on the high seas, and I pray every night for our Good Lord to keep him safe.'

'Well, it's been nice talking to yer, but I have to be going. I've still one or two bits to pack.' She added, 'Mum says she'll leave the washing for another day. But if you wouldn't mind, I'd like you to come with me mum, to see me off at the station.'

'Will the boys be there?' I asked.

'No, they're on day shift. But I've already said my goodbyes.'

The railway station was packed with soldiers, sailors and airmen. Nurses and young women in uniform, too, stood sadly waiting for the train, and as it slowly puffed its way into the station everyone began to kiss and wave their loved ones goodbye, and after Sal had hugged and kissed her daughter, Florrie threw her arms round me and whispered, 'Look after me mum for me, and will you write and let me know how things go?'

'I will,' I replied, as she kissed her mum and me again.

As she managed to squeeze her head through the window and wave, our tears began to fall. Everyone cried – I don't believe there was a dry eye on that platform the day that overcrowded train pulled out of New Street Station.

Sal was very upset after saying goodbye to her daughter that Monday morning, so I thought it best that I should stay with her until her sons came home from work.

As soon as I had seen my two young daughters off to work, I went into her house and made a pot of tea. When we had drunk it Sal seemed to be more herself, yet I could still see she'd been crying. I knew she always cheered up after a drink of whisky, so I went back indoors and helped myself to a drop from what the warden had left.

'This will have to be the last, Sal,' I said, 'otherwise Mr Smith will want to know who's been helping themselves, and I can't lie to him.'

'But I thought it was yowers,' she replied.

'No, Sal, we had the last of that the other night. Anyway, I wish we *did* have a drop more; the way I feel I could drink a whole bottle.'

'Well, if yo'll look in me cupboard yo'll find half a bottle of Scotch in there.'

'You crafty old bugger, and there's me sneaking a drop from the warden's bottle!'

As I put the half-bottle on the table, she said, 'I worn't 'idin' it, Kate. I was savin' it fer when Tom cums 'ome – if 'e does cum back. Any'ow, 'im bein' a Catholic 'e only likes Irish, so 'ere goes, pour it out, Kate.'

I poured out two little tumblers and we drank it up neat. Now that I felt the whisky was loosening our tongues, I said, 'I didn't know your husband was a Catholic, you never said.'

'It's only 'im that's Irish, but 'e wanted me an' me children ter change our religion an' become Catholics, but we're Protestants an' alwis will be. And that was the beginnin' of our troubles, an' when 'e wanted me in bed 'e often used ter say, "Sal me darlin', you'd mek a foine good Irishwoman," but I never did believe any of 'is blarney, an' yer know what, 'e was very lustful an' all, 'e'd 'ave 'ad it anywhere, mornin' noon an' night – that's if I'd 'ave let 'im; an' when I wouldn't sleep with 'im, that's when 'e started ter knock me about, an' many times 'e'd come 'ome drunk and swear at me.'

'But what did your sons say about him?'

'They worn't born then. It was just after 'e sold that old cottage what belong to 'is old mum, an' soon after, we came ter live 'ere. 'E wouldn't give me any money fer food or rent so I found meself a job in a rivetin' factory. After a while 'e began ter alter 'is ways, an' 'e said if I dain't let 'im 'ave 'is oats 'e'd turn me out an' get another woman in. So I eventually slept with 'im to cause peace. But when I found I was pregnant agen, I dain't know what ter do, an' when the girls in the factory said 'ow pale I was, I wouldn't say why. But when they found out, one of them said, "Yer wanta goo ter the chemist an' ask 'im ter mek yer up a box of the four Ps." When I asked what she meant, she said I must be green. They was called Dr Williams' Pink Pills for Pale People.'

Suddenly Sal began to laugh: 'I can laugh now, Kate, when I think about the time I took them pills. But I dain't laugh at the time. They nearly finished me off. Any'ow I was so desperate, after tekin' two, four times a day, they made no effect. So I bought another box and swallowed the whole lot.'

'Oh my Lord, you never did!' I exclaimed.

'I did,' she replied. 'But they only gave me the shits, an' I 'ad ter run down the factory yard ter the outside closet every few minutes, and when the foreman saw me 'e 'ad me in 'is office an' when I told 'im, 'e give me the sack. I was ill in 'ospital for over a week, but all the sympathy I got off Tom, bein' a Catholic, was if I'd 'ave bin a Catholic I could 'ave gone ter confession an' 'ad me sins forgiven by Father O'Murphy. But the worst of it was, I was still pregnant, an' when I told Tom, 'e forgive me. But while I was in the 'ospital, I lost the babby, an' Tom was frightened then that 'e'd lose me too.'

'You ain't had a very happy life even from the beginning, Sal. But why did yer marry him?' I added.

'I 'ad no other choice, Kate. When 'is old mother died, it was either be thrown out or sleep with 'im, an' I've regretted it ever since.'

'But you must have loved him to marry him later.'

'I dain't luv 'im, Kate, but 'e was good ter me at times and I thought it was fer the best – yer see I dain't want *my* children to grow up to be called bastards.'

'I understand, Sal. I could never say I really loved the father of my children. But it was a way out for me too – so I thought at the time. I was a drudge and a lackey when I was only a schoolgirl, I did everything to please my mum, but she was cruel and unkind to me, and in later years I found I wasn't wanted, even before I was born. She liked the sweets, but never liked the sours, if yer know what I mean,' I replied, smiling.

'Even when I was at school I had big ideas, and wanted to grow up quickly and get married and have lots of babies. I thought that was the only way to be happy. But like an ignorant fool, I met my handsome feller at a party, we'd had a few drinks, then one night we made love in an entry. I was then nearly eighteen and knew nothing of the facts of life, and when I found out I was pregnant, I was glad. Foolishly I thought, now he had to ask me to get married, I would have a home of my own, away from my mum and the squalid surroundings we lived in. But this was not to be – my first disappointment was when I went to live with him in Bath Row, before we got married, but when the landlady turned us out we went to live in a furnished room, and when I was three months pregnant my husband lost his job. Times were bad for almost everyone in the district in 1921, I couldn't pay the rent that was overdue. There was only one alternative. When I asked my mother if I could come to live back home until my baby was born she said, "No! Yo've med yer bed, so yer lie on it!" But after my dad discussed the situation we were in, she changed her mind. Believe me, Sal, that was the last place I wanted to go, but beggars can't be choosers. And that's where all my future hopes collapsed. My husband lost his job – as yer know, jobs were hard to find – and when he started to sell sawdust to the butchers and the pubs, he often came home drunk, and when he came home the worse for drink and wanted me in bed, I refused to even sleep beside him. He never came near me for months after we quarrelled. When he was sober, I longed for him to make love to me, but after walking the streets all day looking for work he was too tired even to have a conversation. One night while he was out, I dragged the zinc bath indoors and as I lay in the hot carbolic soapy water, I was scared in case the water got into my navel and drowned my baby. I was ignorant regarding childbirth. So I got a piece of sticking plaster and stuck it over my navel. As soon as I got out of the bath, I stood wet and naked in front of the long mirror, and when I removed the plaster, I felt wonderful and happy about this little life that was growing in my little swollen belly, and as I put my hand there I hoped to feel it move, then I suddenly saw my husband looking at me. I wanted him so badly, then, to take me in his arms and make love to me. But as he stared at me, you know what he said? "Yer betta put some clothes on, before yer catch cold", and he walked out.

'That was many years ago, Sal, and God knows how often I'd pray for things to change so that I could get away from that squalid district and rapidly increasing families. But my prayers were never answered, until ten years later in 1931 when my husband died.'

As I was telling her some of my life story, I noticed Sal was becoming *too* inquisitive. It was then that I realised my tongue had run away with me. 'I'll have to be going, Sal,' I replied at once. 'It's getting late and my daughters will be home for their tea.'

I had previously told her that I was leaving Waverhill Road to my eldest daughter Kathleen, as I had already bought a house in the select district of Handsworth. No doubt when I had gone she would find time to gossip with her other neighbour, Mrs Freer. I had nothing to hide or be ashamed of, yet I didn't like neighbours' gossip, and I don't know why I should have talked as I did. Therefore when she did ask questions, I would say, 'When we have more time' until she got tired of asking. But we were still neighbourly, and I felt sorry for her at times, so I did many kindnesses for her. But it wasn't until a few days before I was leaving the district that I realised she had been taking advantage of my kindness in little things she asked me to do, and I never refused.

# Georgie's Superstitious Accident

One day Sal came to ask if I'd keep an eye on her little son Georgie, as she'd heard there was some extra sausages to be had at the butcher's. 'I'll bring yer some, Kate, if they ain't sold out afower I get there,' she replied.

'Thanks, Sal,' I replied. 'Don't bother if yer can't get me any, but you can bring Georgie in.'

Georgie sat down, and as soon as Sal hurried away, I asked him if he'd like a game of dominoes. We had a happy half-hour together. He was a lovable little chap but when I saw the disappointment on his face when he lost the first game, I let him win the other two.

'Me bruvvers said I don't know 'ow ter play properly, but wait till I tell 'em,' he gloated, smiling all over his face.

As soon as we started the next game, there was a knock on the door. When I opened it, little Jimmy from down the street cried, 'Me mum ses Georgie's in your 'ouse, can 'e come out an' play?'

When I told Georgie his friend had come for him, he said, 'Can I goo now? 'E wants me ter play with 'is trains.'

'Very well, but you must be here when yer mum comes back.'

Jimmy was the little lad across the street, and I'd heard that no one knew who his father was, not even his mother. And in that close community, everybody knew everybody else's business. She was known to go away, leaving him to roam the streets for weekends at a time, and when the boy was born everyone knew he was a bastard. Many neighbours used to shun her when the Yanks came to town, yet some fallen girls had mothers who understood when their daughters were left holding their babies. Other mothers just could never find time to forgive. Yet today, thousands of children are born out of wedlock, and couples just live together without marriage.

Sal came back two hours later with no sausages, in quite a temper. 'Two bleedin' hours I stood in that queue. An' when it cum ter my turn 'e said 'e'd only some scratchin's left. I told 'im where 'e could stick 'is scratchings – where the monkey sticks 'is nuts, up 'is arse!'

I began to laugh, then she said, 'An' yer know what 'e said – if I'd goo round the back 'e'd push 'em up mine! Saucy bleeder!' she exclaimed.

When she asked where Georgie was, I told her he was playing with Jimmy. Later that same afternoon, it had been raining heavily when Sal came knocking on my door, dragging little Georgie behind her. As soon as they entered I noticed that his knee was covered in blood and there was mud all over his face and hands, and he was sobbing.

'Whatever have you done?' I cried as I gazed down at him.

''E won't say, Kate. I carn't get a word outa 'im!' yelled Sal as she shook him. 'All as I can get out of 'im is 'e fell down.'

'Well, Georgie, let me have a look an' see what you've done.'

I sat him down on a chair, and got a bowl of water and some salt. When I bathed the mud and blood from his knees, I saw that on his left leg there was quite a deep cut.

When I asked how he'd done it, he replied, 'I fell over.'

'Georgie,' I replied, 'you're not telling the truth, are you?'

'I am, I fell over in the mud,' he replied as he began to sob.

'Trouble, trouble!' his mum cried out. 'I don't know what I'm gooin' ter do with 'im.'

'You'll have to take him to the hospital, Sal,' I snapped. 'It's a bad cut he's got there.'

'I carn't tek 'im, Kate, I'm scared of 'ospitals.'

'So am I!' I replied angrily. 'Anyway, I'll take him to see Dr Arthur first and let him have a look at it.'

When she said she would come along too, I replied, 'No need for the two of us, it may not be all that serious. Anyway, if my daughter Jean comes home before I get back, just tell her where I've gone.'

As soon as the doctor saw Georgie he said, 'Now come along, young man, and let me sponge them dirty tears away, then when I've looked at your knee you can tell me how it happened.'

'I fell down,' he whimpered.

'But that's not all, is it, Georgie? Have you been fighting?' he asked.

'Oh no, I worn't fightin' an' that's the truth, Doctor.'

Suddenly he began to cry again.

'Now wipe your eyes and tell me how you cut your knee.'

'I told yer, I fell down in the mud, an' that's the truth.'

The doctor, like me, was getting nowhere, but after he'd cleaned the cut, he said I was to take the boy to the hospital.

Georgie was a brave little chap. He had two stitches in that cut and never murmured, and the doctor said I was to report back to him. As soon as we left the hospital, I took him to my home before taking him to his mum, and after giving him a drink of warm milk I said, 'Now Georgie, if you'll tell me what really happened, I'll get the dominoes out and we'll have a game.'

'Will yer promise not ter tell me mum or me bruvvers?' he asked.

'Why?' I asked.

'Becuss they'll belt me.'

'No they won't, Georgie,' I replied. 'Anyway, if you tell me what really happened, I'll keep it a secret, but I can't promise until you tell me.'

As soon as I handed him a hanky to wipe his tears, he said, 'Yer know Jimmy, well, 'e tells lies.'

'Do you tell lies, Georgie?' I asked.

'No, Mrs Flood,' he replied, 'only little white fibs, but Jimmy does.'

Now I'd got him talking. I sat and listened.

'When it stopped rainin' we went for a walk alung the canal bank and 'e told me . . . er . . . er . . .'

'Go on, Georgie, he told you what?' I asked, smiling at him.

''E told me, if yer stared at a cross-eyed woman it was bad luck, but if yer stared at a crossed-eyed man it brought yer good luck, an' then yer could wish for anythink an' it would come true, but Jimmy told me a lie and, and . . . er . . .'

'Yes, go on, and what else did Jimmy say?'

'As we was walkin' along the bridge we saw this cockeyed woman, an' Jimmy ran away and left me.'

'And what did you do?' I asked.

'When she cum nearer I got frightened an' run away.'

He didn't seem to want to tell me any more, for I could see he was beginning to cry again.

I wiped his eyes. 'Now, Georgie,' I said, smiling down at him, 'you don't want to cry. I only want you to tell me how you came to cut your knee, then we can have a game of dominoes like I promised.'

And so he went on telling me. He was on his way home when he met a cross-eyed man. 'So I went straight up to him and stared at 'im, then when 'e asked me what I was starin' at, I told 'im that my friend Jimmy said it was lucky ter stare up at a cockeyed man. Then 'e said, "Well, yer can 'ave this fer luck," then he hit me twice across me face, then knocked me down in the mud an' I fell on some broken glass. An' I'll never believe anythink Jimmy tells me again.'

'Well, Georgie, they're all silly superstitions and if anyone tells you anything you don't understand, just ask your mum or your brothers to explain, they're the ones to put you right. Now come along, we've got to go back and report to the doctor. Then we'll come back and play dominoes.'

I took hold of his hand and off we went. On the way he said, 'Please don't tell me mum nor the doctor.'

'I won't,' I replied.

A few days later, when I called to see the doctor about my chest cold, he asked if the lad had confided in me. I saw no reason why I should *not* tell him, and when I did, he began to smile.

'The things these lads say and do surprises even me. Anyway,' he added, 'he's maybe learnt his lesson.'

Superstitions die hard as they're handed down from one generation to the next.

I remember my mum was very superstitious. If there was a storm brewing and lightning about, she was like a woman demented. She'd jump up from wherever she was sitting and face the mirror to the wall, and knives and forks would be suddenly snatched up from the table, whether you were having your dinner or not, and slung underneath, also the steel poker from the fireplace.

'Don't you dare open that umbrella in the 'ouse!' she'd yell.

And to crack the mirror was seven years' bad luck. There are a thousand and one silly superstitions – if you walked under a ladder, that was said to be bad luck, but it was bad luck if you stepped off the pavement and got knocked down by a horse. You could also hear people swearing every day, but not on a Sunday, otherwise the Devil would be with you the rest of the week.

I also recall my mum would never wear green, nor have it anywhere in the house. I didn't know about this until one Christmas. I'd tried to save up a few shilling to buy Mum a present. When the 'pat man' (the hire-purchase man) came to the door and showed me a green chenille tablecloth, I hadn't got enough money, but he said I could have it on the 'strap' for sixpence a week, and with the promise to pay sixpence I gave him the first instalment. I thought it would look lovely on our scrubbed wooden table – make a change from the pages from the *News of the World* (so I thought), but as soon as I gave the parcel to her and she saw what was inside she went wild and threw it on the fire.

I was shocked, but before I could say a word she yelled out, 'If yo ever bring anythink green in this 'ouse again, it'll still goo on the fire!' Then all of a sudden the room lit up, as we saw the chimney had caught fire. Balls of soot came rolling down, and the room was full of smoke. Just then my dad came running with bags of salt to push up the chimney, but we hadn't had it swept for years. The old chimney was alight – flames, sparks and smoke were belching out into the yard below as we ran outside. We heard the pot crack. The firemen came and a couple of policemen, but all Mum could do was tell the neighbours and swear as she helped to drag in the washing off the lines.

Later, Mum was fined half-a-crown, and I still had to pay that sixpence a week to the 'pat man', until four and eleven-pence three farthings was paid.

I swore after that episode I would never buy her anything green. In fact, I never bought her anything else either.

Yet today green is one of my favourite colours.

It was during the spring that the landlord decided to have all the doors painted in the yard (which he did once in a blue moon). My mum happened to be out at the time, and when she came back later and saw the door painted green, she went wild. She rushed over to the brewhouse and helped herself to a bucket of warm soapsuds from the boiler, and as she got the bass broom all the neighbours came out to see her perform. But try as she might with that broom, the paint wouldn't budge. Suddenly she lost her temper and threw the rest of the suds against the door. Next day, when the landlord came for his rent, she yelled out, 'Yow'll get no bleedin' rent off me, till yer get that green paint off me dower an' put another colour on!'

She meant it, too. But when he threatened her with the bailiffs, Dad said he'd paint it over. Dad was no painter, but he managed to beg a tin of brown paint, and after thinning it down he too lost his temper and slapped it anywhere. And our door was the only one in that street that had smudgy brown and green streaks. Often I used to imagine I could picture figures and faces where that paint had dried, and it was left like that from when I was only a young girl until Hitler decided he didn't like it either and destroyed it in 1941.

# Lambs to the Slaughter

During May 1945 the war was nearing its end and there was less bombing, if any at all, over Birmingham.

During these times we could go to our beds and try to catch up on the many hours of sleep we had lost during the heavy raids. I was still living in Waverhill Road with my daughters, but I had every intention of leaving for a better house in a much quieter district as soon as the war was over.

I remember that my kitchen was very small and the door opened inwards, so it always banged against the wall. I thought if I could get someone to rehang it so that it opened outwards, that would give me a bit more room in the kitchen.

A friend of mine said he could do the job for me, but that I would have to have a new door as the old one was warped. He also said it would be a long time before he could get a new one as he would have to get a priority note, but he could get one from a bomb site. He got a very heavy door, made of oak. After he had planed it down it fitted, and after a lot of hard work and strong language he managed to make it swing outwards, and I had a bit more room. We didn't realise it was now going to be a tight squeeze to get outside between the door and the wall in the entry, yet my two daughters and I managed somehow. It was more of a squeeze for me – I was then twelve stone. But we said that now the door was up it could stay until such time as we left.

A few weeks later, I was surprised to see my brother-in-law Bill. He worked for a butcher in Handsworth, fetching and carrying meat from the markets in his van.

'Hello, stranger!' I cried as I opened the front door and saw his meat van outside. 'Come in.'

'I can't stop long, Kate,' he replied. 'But I happened to be passing, so I thought I'd call and see if yer wanted a bit of lamb.'

'Thank yer, Bill, but I ain't got any coupons to spare,' I said.

'That's OK. I've got some to spare if yer want the meat.'

'All right, bring it in then,' I answered eagerly.

'I ain't got any with me now, but I'll drop yer some in a day or two. So long, I've gotta 'urry now,' he added as he went out.

After I had thanked him and watched him drive away, I wondered if I'd done the right thing by accepting the lamb he'd promised. On second thoughts, I said to myself, if he did bring some it would only be maybe a few chops.

A couple of weeks went by. No Bill came with any lamb, so I forgot about it. I was glad really, I knew it was on the black market, but I made up my mind that if he did come now I wouldn't accept it, for I was scared I would be found out.

A few nights later I was awakened by noises which sounded like bombs being dropped, a long way off. Half asleep, I sat up in bed waiting for the sirens to wail. I heard a loud thud, then another, and another, which seemed to sound much nearer. I sat up in bed now, wide awake, thinking the sirens would sound any time, but there was no more noise, so I lay down and tried to go back to sleep. But I was too restless. It was almost dawn when I decided to go downstairs. As I slipped my dressing-gown on and lit the gas stove to make myself a cup of tea, I looked up at the clock. It was five-thirty.

It was very stuffy and warm as I stood waiting for the kettle to boil. I thought I'd unbolt the door and let in some air. When I tried to push the door outwards it wouldn't budge. I put my shoulder to it, but still it wouldn't budge. I knew then that something was blocking it. Suddenly I became scared in case it was a delayed bomb, but I had to get outside to see. I went out through the front door and round the back towards the passageway, hoping and praying that someone would be walking along the street, and would come with me to see who or what was lying there. But there wasn't a soul in sight; everywhere seemed deadly quiet.

Warily I crept up to the back of my house, and when I got almost to the back door I couldn't believe my eyes. Wedged between my kitchen door and the wall were three whole lambs. I had to step on them and push them against the wall before I could get the door open.

I was relieved to see that none of my neighbours was about, but I had to hide those lambs somewhere. I managed to drag each one into the kitchen, and after closing the door I sat down exhausted. I had to get them into the cellar somehow and hide them from my daughters. After drinking my welcome cup of tea, I went to my peg bag and found an odd piece of rope. I tied it round each lamb's neck and dragged them towards the cellar steps. As soon as I reached the edge of the steps I unfastened the rope and pushed them down.

I had expected that Bill would show himself with a few chops, or a half a leg, not *three whole bloody lambs!* Whatever was I going to do with them? I was more scared now than if they had been a dud bomb.

But as luck would have it, half an hour later my brother Jack called.

When I told him about my brother-in-law and what he'd left me with, he began to laugh.

'It's no bloody laughin' matter, Jack!' I yelled. 'What am I goin' ter do with 'em?'

'Well,' he replied, still grinning all over his face, 'I'll tek 'em away, I'll soon get rid of 'em.'

I didn't care what he did with them as long as they were out of the house. So it was arranged that the three lambs would stay where I had pushed them until after dark, when Jack would take them away in his car.

When he came later that night, he said he had room for only two and he'd call later to pick up the other one. Soon after he left, my brother-in-law called. As soon as I opened the door I yelled out 'Yer better come in and explain yerself!'

He looked around and asked, 'Wot yer done with 'em?'

'What yer think I've done with em!' I replied angrily. 'I had to throw 'em down the cellar.'

Smiling, he said, 'Well, I'll tek the two and leave yer the other one.'

'I don't want it! And if yer think yer can use me or my house for any of yer dirty deals, you've got another think coming!'

Suddenly his smile changed when I told him my brother had taken two of them away and was coming back later for the other one.

''E won't, yer know! Not if I can 'elp it. I'll tek the one 'e's left fer now, an' I'll see *'im* later!'

He was fuming as he made his way down into the cellar. As soon as he had put the lamb into a sack and began to throw it into the van, I shouted, 'This is the first an' last time yer try ter use me for your black-market deals!'

Later my brother came, expecting to take the other lamb away, but when I told him what had happened he replied, ''E won't bother me, Kate, 'e knows we're in the same boat. But', he added, 'if yer want a few chops, I'll . . .'

'Yer know what yer can do with yer chops! You and 'im! Keep away from my house. I never wanta see you nor 'im again!' I bawled as I slammed the door behind him.

I never saw my brother-in-law again, and only very seldom did I see my brother Jack.

# Sweet William and the Copycat

Ration books were more precious than identity cards. Clothes, food and vegetables were still rationed years after the war was over. Many people who were lucky enough to own a garden made good use of it by growing their own vegetables. Children, too, would help to dig and carry buckets of water after school hours. When my two brothers came back from the war they rented their houses, dug up the soil and grew their own too. Prizes were given by the Co-op Corporation Society for the best-laid-out gardens.

We were all proud when my brothers won first and third prizes. I don't know where they got their knowledge from.

As far back as I remember when we were children, we had only a cobbled yard. The only green we ever saw were the weeds between the blue bricks and pitch between the cobbles. Many of us young kids in our district walked miles to see trees and flowers, even a patch of grass.

Often I used to wish my mum would have the bailiffs and go to another house with a garden, but this was not to be. For I loved plants and flowers, and still do in my old age. When I was about five years old, I had this crazy notion that I could grow anything in a bit of soil. Once I planted a brown marble in the corner of the yard, hoping it would grow into many. After a few weeks I dug the soil over, but all I could see was that it had perished. Next I decided to pull up one of the bricks in the corner of the yard. I had a few bluebells I'd picked while out walking. I turned the dirt over, buried them and poured water on them every night. But one day, when I went to look, there was nothing there, only bits of dead leaves. Often my brother would tease me and laugh and tell me I must have planted them upside down. When he saw my tears, he said, 'Never mind, Katie, one day when yer rich and yer goo to Australia, you'll find they've med their way and shot up there.'

Often on my walks I would still pick bluebells or buttercups and put them in jars of water, but they never lasted more than a couple of days before they too drooped and died on me.

Yet I had my reward. One day, as I stood gazing in the window of a flower shop, I couldn't take my eyes away from the beautiful plants and flowers arranged in pretty vases. As I stood there, wondering if I would ever be able to own a shop like that, the old flower-seller beckoned me to come inside. I was scared at first, for I had no money to buy even a leaf. But as soon as I stepped inside the shop, he said, 'You've been standing there for a long time, my dear, do you want to buy your mum something?'

'No,' I replied at once. 'I ain't got any money, but I love to look at your lovely flowers,' I added nervously.

He said he was sorry, but he couldn't afford to give me any. But as I went to walk out of the shop, he called me back. 'Well, dear,' he said kindly, 'would you like a packet of seeds? Then you can grow your own.'

'But I ain't even got a penny,' I replied.

'Well, dear, I'll give you a packet and you can bring me the penny another time.'

'Thank you, sir, thank you, sir,' I cried as I took the packet and ran out of the shop before he changed his mind.

When I got home, I didn't tell my mum – I hid the seeds in case she threw them away or on the fire. Yet I had no idea where I was going to plant them, and I didn't want them shooting up in Australia. So I thought the best thing was to give them to my dad, who might give them to somebody to grow for me.

Then one day I told him about the kind man at the flower shop and when I showed him the packet of seeds, he said, 'Well, luv, I don't know where yer gooin' ter grow 'em, any'ow leave 'em with me an' I'll see what I can do.'

A few days later, I saw him making a long narrow wooden box for the window-ledge, and when it was finished he not only gave me the penny to pay the flower-seller, he also bought a bag of compost.

As he planted the seeds into the soil and watered them down, I hugged and kissed him as he stood back to admire his handiwork. How proud I was now to have my own private little flowerbox! Just as we were admiring it, Mum happened to come back from her cleaning job. I was afraid she'd take it down. As soon as she set eyes on it, she cried, 'What's that monstrosity you've nailed on theea?'

'Yer won't call it a monstrosity', Dad replied, 'when yer see the sweet williams shootin' up.'

'Well, as lung as yer don't paint that box green,' she said, as she shrugged her shoulders and went indoors. Dad smiled and winked at me, for we both remembered the commotion when she tried to scrub the green paint off the door.

Every day I used to peer down into that soil to see if any little shoot had broken through. But when my mum caught me, she said, 'Yer must be barmy! Starin' at nothin'.! Get in the 'ouse, where I can find yer summat betta ter do!'

I knew she didn't want that flowerbox on the window-ledge. She never encouraged me at any time to do something *I* wanted to. Only my dad had patience with me.

One morning I was very happy to see several little shoots peeping through the soil, and when my dad saw them he too was proud to see what a success he'd made. From then on I had my own private little flowerbox, which I called *my* garden.

When the flowers began to flourish and show colour, all the neighbours who passed our door admired them, except the one neighbour at the end of the yard. Her name was Maggie, but everybody called her Moggy, because she had lots of cats. Mum never liked her and she didn't like our mum, especially when her mangy cats kept coming into our house – Mum would kick them out. But there was one big old ginger tom whose mangy fur would bristle and stand on end and defy her. Mum had to get the steel poker to *that* one, before he turned tail.

Whenever Maggie saw Mum take the curtains down to

wash, she had to do the same. Even when Mum swilled out the dry wooden closets, or the yard, out would come *her* broom and bucket, and each Saturday morning Mum would whiten our well-worn-down step with a ball of whitening, and when any of us came in or out of the house, we were given our orders *not* to tread on the step, but to stride over it. This too Maggie copied. Yet when the rest of the neighbours did theirs, Mum seemed pleased to see that it improved the look of the yard.

One morning Mum got me out of bed very early, just as dawn was breaking. When I asked why, she replied, 'I wanta get inta that brew'ouse! Afower that bleedin' Moggy wakes up!' But while we were filling the two buckets from the standpipe in the yard, Mum happened to look up. As soon as she saw Maggie staring down at her from the open window, she cried out for all the neighbours to hear, ''Ave yer bin standin' theea all night, yer nosy old cow?'

Suddenly the window shook as Maggie slammed it down. Mum went into the house and slammed the door, leaving me to shiver in the cold morning air.

There was no washing done that day by either of them, none until later that week.

There was only one brewhouse for all five back-to-back houses, so neighbours had to do their washing in pairs. Mum hated to do her washing standing beside Maggie. Often she would ask a neighbour if they would change over, but they always refused. They didn't get along with Moggy either. And when Mum had to do the washing standing beside her, neither spoke a word – they were like a couple of deaf mutes as they banged away with the 'dollies' at the washing in the maiding tubs.

Every time I saw Maggie stop to look at my flowers growing in the windowbox, I would see her sniff and shrug her shoulders.

A few days later I saw her dragging a wet fishbox down the yard. Being an inquisitive child, I stood to watch her. Other times she would shoo me off, but she took no notice of me as I watched her pull it apart and try to codge four pieces together with a few nails and a hammer. As it took shape I realised she was trying to make a windowbox. As soon as it was finished, she placed in on the window-ledge and filled it with some kind of dirt and soil. When Mum came out of doors and saw her sprinkling seeds into it, she cried, 'What yer think yower growing in theea, Moggy?'

'Not sweet williams!' she yelled back. 'Mine will be sweet peas!' she added, tossing her head.

Suddenly Mum burst out laughing and yelled, 'The only sweet peas yo'll grow in theea will be the sweet pees from yower mangy tom cats!'

True enough, a few weeks later she pulled it down. After throwing the dirt in the dustbin, she chopped the box up for firewood. She never made another attempt.

# Joe

My first place that I rented in Albert Road was 12s. 6d a week. I was in my seventh heaven when I began to furnish it ready for my daughters to come home to.

We were all happy together for a while, and now my business was thriving. I felt I wanted a better house, yet I couldn't make up my mind until the bombing started. Then I bought an old house in Waverhill Road, and as soon as we moved in, I heard that the house I had rented was bombed.

Kath and Jean soon settled into our new home, and after leaving work they would go out with some of the girls who worked for me. Yet I always had the feeling (like all mothers do) that they were growing away from me. Sometimes they would ask me to accompany them and we would have friends and neighbours in for parties and share our food rations. Yet as soon as they began to grow up during those teenage years, my trials began, for I now had to cope with a grown-up family. Although I gave them love and affection I believe I gave too much, too soon. I didn't stop to think that one day they would leave me to get married and have a home and children of their own. I thought the time to worry would be the time when they left me.

Then one day I had a letter from my son John, who was on leave in Scotland, to say he'd fallen in love with a Scots girl and was going to get married. He was only young. He knew no other life than the time he was at Watts Naval Training School, and he was only fifteen years old when he was shipped out to sea.

I went to see them both married in Scotland, taking my two elder daughters with me.

A couple of visits later, while we were there, my eldest

daughter fell in love with a Scotsman. Later they were married from my home and went back to live in Scotland.

Mary, my youngest, was still evacuated, which now left only Jean and me at home, and sometimes life together was difficult.

Nothing ever seemed to go the way I had planned it. The war was at its height, more or less every town had its share of bombings, and later, when I heard that my mother and eldest sister had been killed in an air raid, I began to have feelings that this old house was unlucky. But then I thought maybe it was my silly superstition and I was being foolish.

Nevertheless, when I had a letter from Kathleen and her husband Jim to say they wanted to come back to Birmingham, I decided to leave the house in Waverhill Road to them.

The next house I bought was a semi-detached with a garage, a front lawn, and a large garden at the back. There was also a large pool that ran at the back of the houses and many frogs on the lawn, but these didn't bother me. Jean and I settled down and we grew closer together – until she too started courting. I was left alone at night in this house, where I had foolishly thought I'd never be alone again. I imagined all kinds of strange noises and creaks, especially when I slept alone in my bed. I began to think: was it mice – I could hear scratching – or was the house haunted? Later I had my doubts.

During those war years I had become very nervous and imagined all kinds of things when I was alone. Often, lying awake at night, I used to think: would I feel better with a man around the house? Should I advertise for a male lodger? But on second thoughts, my next-door neighbours knew I was a widow, and knowing how they loved to gossip, I thought it wouldn't be a good idea; anyhow, I knew my Jean would object.

A few nights later, as I sat knitting and waiting for my daughter to come home, I glanced up at the clock and saw it was almost half-past ten. She had gone to the pictures with her boyfriend, Sam. Although I knew I could trust him to bring her home safely, I still worried until she was indoors.

It was while I was waiting that I heard the front doorbell ring. I knew it couldn't be Jean, she had her own key. I thought it must be one of my neighbours, asking if we had seen their cat, for Jean was a lover of any kind of animal and always picked up a stray and brought it home, saying it had followed her. If I had given her the chance, our house would have been a menagerie.

When I opened the door, I was surprised to see a young man dressed in sergeant's air force uniform. I peeped outside to see if my nosy neighbour was about before I invited him inside. I didn't recognise him at first, but as soon as he told me his name I knew him at once. He was the young man who had taken me to the Lyric picture house when we were teenagers, many years before.

'Sit down, Joe – would you like a cup of coffee or tea?' I asked as I began to smile, remembering that night.

'Tea, thank you, Kate,' he replied.

I was still smiling as I handed him his cup. When he asked me why, I answered, 'I still remember the night you took me to the pictures, and bought me a large box of Rowntree's chocolates. And do you remember when you pulled me towards you and tried to kiss me?'

'Yes, I still remember – you slapped my face and threw the box at me and ran off,' said Joe, smiling.

'Did you finish eating them?'

'No, I gave them to the usherette and went to find *you* to say I was sorry, but you seemed to vanish, and I never saw you again.'

'But how did you find me now?' I asked.

'I met your brother and he gave me your address. I hope you don't mind, Kate.'

'No, Joe, I'm glad to see you again,' I replied.

'Anyway, I'll have to be going, I've got to see my dad. Would you mind if I call again, Kate, and take you out for a drink and a meal?'

'No, Joe, I'd love that,' I replied eagerly.

As he said good night and left, I didn't know that this meeting was going to be the beginning of a long friendship.

He had been gone only a few seconds when I heard the key turn in the lock and Jean came in. Almost at once she cried, 'Who's that air force man I just seen leaving here?'

'It's a long story, Jean,' I replied. 'Just someone I met when I was a young girl.'

'But what brought him here? Did you invite him?' she asked, staring at me as though I had kept a secret from her.

'No I did not! Even if I did, I don't see why you have to question me about who I see. Now get your supper, I'm waiting to go to bed.'

'I don't want any supper,' she snapped, and bounced her way upstairs.

I could see she was in a mood and I put it down to a lovers' quarrel.

No more was said. Next night she got herself ready to meet Sam. When he called I greeted him, and not long after they left Joe came to take me out for a meal.

I remember I had a wonderful time. I met his dad and his sisters, and when we had said our goodbyes Joe brought me home. As we sat talking about my family and his family, time seemed to fly.

Before he left he took me in his arms, and we were kissing just as Jean came into the room.

'How long 'as this been going on?' she cried.

Before I could answer she shrugged her shoulders and went up to her room.

'I'm sorry, Joe, Jean feels this way, she thinks I shouldn't have anyone in the house when she's not here.'

'I understand, Kate, don't let it bother you. One day when she gets wed she'll come to realise how lonely life can be for you without her.'

Jean and I never spoke to each other for days. When Joe asked me to marry him, I agreed.

As soon as I told my daughter she yelled, 'But yer can't, Mum! He's already married!'

'I know, Jean, he's only waiting for his divorce papers, then we're going to the registry office to get married.'

'Don't ask me to be there when you do get married!' she replied quickly.

'I'm not asking *you* to do anything you don't want to do, Jean, but remember this: I don't want to hear any more about what I should do or not do, from you or anyone else,' I said angrily.

As soon as she went out I began to weep. If only she could see my point of view and know the lonely hours I spent alone in that house!

I was surprised to see her come home early that night with Sam, who left her to talk with me. As soon as I looked at her, I could see she'd been crying. Before I could say a word, she threw her arms around me and cried, 'I'm sorry, Mum, I've been angry with you. Sam has explained everything to me, and made me feel ashamed.'

'There's nothing for you to be ashamed of, Jean. I shall always love you no matter what happens. But you must realise that I have always put you, Kath, John and Mary first. I could have married again years ago but I was too busy building a home and getting a business together for all our comforts. But fate intervened in other ways. Now wipe your eyes – you're a pretty girl, you don't want to go to work with red swollen eyes.'

We kissed and as I put my arms around her she said, 'I'm sorry, Mum, but I do love you. It's only because I want to see you happy.'

'I'm sure I will be, Jean. But you must understand, when you and Sam get married I should have been left alone again, and you . . .'

'But we'll always come and visit you, Mum, and bring you anything you need.'

'I know you will, love; now let's have a nice cup of cocoa and tell me all about your plans for the future.'

'We haven't made any yet, Mum. But we'll tell you when we do. Anyway, Sam sends his love and I'm glad, Mum, he made me see sense.'

A few weeks later, Joe and I were married at the old

registry office in Edmund Street, near the famous fountain where I used to paddle my sore bare feet as a child.

Joe was usually kind and considerate, and although we had many disagreements, I still loved him.

# 'Sheila'

I realised that my husband was often mean, and at times he was not very easy to get along with. Yet despite meanness he had a sense of humour, which was one of the things I liked about him.

There was one thing I was grateful for: he didn't drink beer, or any kind of alcohol. Tea was his favourite drink.

We had our differences of opinion, as many couples often do, but when he was in one of his *good* moods I only had to ask and he'd give me the money to buy whatever I needed. While we were living in Handsworth, my husband became acquainted with a bookmaker who employed him. But taking bets and staying at his club late at night to pay money out to punters was not my idea of life. It meant I had to be left alone in that house until he came home.

Sitting alone, waiting, I was always nervous, wondering if this old house was haunted, like the previous one we had left. Sometimes I was scared of my own shadow. I'd switch on all the lights, but as soon as I heard him coming down the path I ran and switched them all off.

We had a front room, a dining-room, a small kitchen, and three bedrooms. This house was not centrally heated – our hot water came from the boiler at the back of the fire grate, which supplied us only with hot water from the tap in the kitchen sink. One day, we quarrelled about having central heating installed, but I was adamant.

I filled in all the usual forms, and while I was waiting for the men to come, I decided to turn the spare room (which was on a level with our bedroom) into a bathroom. The other spare room I kept furnished ready for when my youngest daughter Mary came home from the forces.

When the men came they delivered the washbasin, bath

and toilet, but we still had to wait until the plumbers came, which meant we still had to go downstairs to the kitchen sink for a wash, and across the yard to the lavatory. The public baths in Oxhill Road were just round the corner from our house, which was very convenient for the time being.

I was always active, and I seldom felt the cold weather, but my Joe was always complaining about his cold feet. One week we had rain, snow and ice continually, non-stop. Joe decided to buy himself a rubber hot-water bottle. As soon as I saw it I cried, 'Thinkin' of yerself agen – why couldn't yer buy me one?'

'Yer tell me yer never feel the cold,' he replied, smiling across at me.

'Well, I do! When yer come up to bed late and put yer freezin' legs an' feet against me.'

'No need now, I've got me bottle,' he answered, grinning. I knew it was a waste of time to argue.

Every night he was last to come up to bed. Then one night, when I thought he was asleep, I pushed my feet down the bed. I grasped the bottle between my feet and as I smiled to myself I kicked it over to my side. But I felt his hand slide down the bed and fail to find the bottle, then I felt it sliding up my bare thigh.

Suddenly I shot up and shouted at him, 'No yer don't! If yer too mean to buy *me* one, you ain't goin' to use me to get warm!'

'All right, I'll sleep downstairs,' he replied.

It was no use arguing any more.

But he didn't stay long – back he came with a hot refill. I thought: one of these days he'll get that water too hot and the bottle will burst.

Sure enough, I woke up to find the foot of the bed wet – the bottle was leaking.

I screamed at him and threw the bottle on to the floor. 'Now look what's 'appened!'

'Oh, shut up!' he yelled back. ''Tain't my fault the bottle's leaked.'

'Is that all you can say? Well, this is the last time you 'ave a bottle in my bed,' I yelled. I picked up the dripping bottle and, opening the window, I threw it out into the yard below, and went downstairs.

The following night he was very late. I looked at the bedside clock – it was nearly one-thirty and he still hadn't come up to bed. Surely, I thought, he can't still be sulking! I crept downstairs, but he wasn't in his chair or sitting on the couch. I began to get worried. I went into the kitchen, and there I saw him trying to fix a piece of sticking plaster on that bottle.

'How mean can you get!' I cried as I snatched it from him. 'This time it's goin' into the ashbin and if yer want ter get warm I'm going to buy an electric blanket.'

'What for? They're dangerous! You can get electrocuted with one of them!'

'Not if you switch 'em off!' I replied.

'Well *I* ain't buyin' one, I'm quite satisfied with a bottle and if you aren't I'll buy *you* one too.'

'If you do, I'll sleep in the spare room, where I can get a proper night's sleep.'

'You wouldn't, would yer, Kate?' he grinned. 'You always say you're scared to sleep on yer own.'

'What do you care?' I replied angrily. 'Yer come up late and wake me up, trying to lift me nightie, so yer can put yer cold feet on me belly. Even when I turn over yer try pushing 'em up me back. So now I'm going up ter bed an' I'm goin' ter sleep in the spare room, so good night!' I replied angrily.

I snatched up a couple of blankets and left.

As I tried to settle down to sleep, I heard him creep into the room.

'Are you awake, love?' I heard him whisper.

'Yes! Go away and leave me alone!'

'I've brought you up a nice hot cup of tea.'

'I don't want it!'

'Well, come back in the other bed where we can cuddle up an' keep warm.'

'No! I know your cuddle ups.'

'If you'll come back, I'll even do without me water bottle. I *promise*. I only want for us to cuddle up together. I'm cold.'

I suddenly began to feel guilty at the way I had behaved. I drank the tea and followed him back to bed. As we cuddled up close, he broke his promise and we made love.

Next day he gave me the money to buy a blanket. I called at Lewis's Stores in town and bought a full-sized one, before I changed my mind.

On the way home with my purchase, I began to smile to myself, thinking how possessive he'd been with his water bottle. But there won't be any more squabbles about whose side *this* would be on, I said to myself.

I called the blanket 'Sheila', a name I gave to most things I possessed. Joe often used to laugh at me, saying I was crazy.

The first night I put it in the bed, I was pleased he took to it straight away.

I could have said 'I told you so.' But I thought: let sleeping dogs lie.

The trouble was, it was a hard job to wake him up in the mornings. He was always first to bed and last out.

One night a few weeks later, we had a terrific storm. It was lightening, thundering and raining all through the night. For once Joe was already fast asleep when I went upstairs, and the last thing I did after getting undressed and into my nightdress was to take out my teeth, put them in a pint jug of water with a pinch of salt and leave them on the bathroom shelf. Joe knew I had false teeth, but I never let him see me take them out – I would have felt embarrassed.

As soon as I got into bed I heard him snoring like a contented pig. After a few digs and a couple of grunts, he turned on to his side and went quiet.

I picked up my book and tried to finish reading it, but after a while I lost interest. I switched off the bedside lamp, and it wasn't long before I fell asleep.

I don't know how long I'd slept, when a loud clash of thunder woke me up. I shot up in bed and switched on the light. I felt so hot I thought I was suffocating, and as I slung back the bedclothes, a waft of smoke hit me.

Suddenly I flew out of bed. 'Joe, Joe!' I screamed as I shook him. 'Wake up, wake up!'

'What the bloody hell's the matter with yer now?' he cried, glaring up at me. 'Seen a few mower ghosts?'

'No Joe, look!' I shouted, pointing to the foot of the bed. 'The bed's smoulderin'.'

Suddenly he too flew out of bed. 'I told yer what would 'appen as soon as yer bought that bloody "Sheila", as yer call it! Yer run downstairs and bring some water up, while I try to smother it afore it gets alight.'

When I came back with a bowl of water, I could see he had already opened the window and thrown the feather bed into the yard below – 'Sheila' too.

After a few sharp words, we went to sleep in the spare bed.

Early next morning, when I awoke, it was still dark and still raining heavily. I decided to leave Joe asleep and go downstairs to make myself a cup of tea. I was still dithering in my nightie, but first of all I went into the bathroom to put in my teeth. As soon as I looked inside the jug, I saw there was no water – nor my teeth. I was certain I remembered putting them there. I began to think: had somebody or something come in the night and stolen them? I suddenly became frightened. I began to panic, and as my tears fell I ran back into the bedroom and tried to yell through my toothless gums.

'Joe, Joe! Me teef 'ave gone! Somebody's took me teef!'

'What yer mumblin' about now?'

'Me teef, me teef, they've gone!'

'What yer mean, yer teef 'ave gone!' he mimicked. 'You ain't swallowed 'em, 'ave yer? Anyway, where did yer put 'em?'

'In a jug a water in the baffwoom,' I managed to say.

Suddenly he burst out laughing. 'Then they must be still in amongst the feathers when I used that water for the bed.'

I fled downstairs, hoping and praying they hadn't melted. It was still raining when I bent down, put my hand in and felt among the wet feathers. I couldn't feel them anywhere, then suddenly I gave a sigh of relief – I saw my teeth clinging to 'Sheila'.

Apart from a few wet feathers clinging to them, I was pleased to see that my teeth were intact.

It was still thundering and lightning in the distance as I hurried back upstairs. Shivering and sneezing, I managed to brush the wet feathers off my teeth and put them in a fresh jug of water. After changing my wet nightie for a dry one, I decided we had to sleep in the other room. Joe had already had a cup of hot cocoa waiting for me. 'Come on, love, drink this and get into bed before yer catch yer death of cold.'

After drinking the cocoa I got into bed beside him. He put his arms round me, and as we cuddled up close to get warm, he whispered in my ear, 'You and yer teef!' We both saw the funny side and burst out laughing.

Next morning, when I went into our bedroom to clean up the mess, I knew at once: it wasn't 'Sheila's' fault the bed nearly caught fire. I realised I must have forgotten to switch it off before falling asleep.

When I told my husband, he surprised me by saying, 'Never mind, love, I've remembered it's your birthday tomorra. I'll give yer the money to buy another one. But', he added, 'I'll have the switch my side, then I'll be sure to take the plug out. But first, *you'll* have to buy another feather bed.'

The bed would cost *me* several times more than a blanket would cost *him* – I thought how mean he was.

But I didn't argue, in case he changed his mind.

# Married Life

Joe had been a sergeant in the air force during the war. He was stationed in India and South Africa. Often he used to show me his album and tell me about some of the places he visited. He said that one day he would save enough money to take me to South Africa, but he never got round to it.

When he came back to Birmingham, he could never settle down to work inside a factory. He loved giving orders, but couldn't take them.

He had several outdoor jobs, where he could earn himself a bit of extra money on the side, for he loved handling money. At one period he worked on a milk cart delivering milk. When he wasn't able to straighten the books, he told the manager money was still owing from bad payers. Later he was sacked.

The next job was hulking hundredweights of coal around the streets from a horse and cart. That job didn't last long either.

His other job was at Perry Barr Dog Tracks exercising the dogs. One day he brought home 'Hopwas Reward', one of the greyhounds, to show me. It was his favourite, but when I saw its ribs showing through its skin I asked, 'What do yer feed 'em on to win a race? Starve 'em?' I added.

'No, they have to be on a special diet.'

'I don't know about callin' 'im "Hopwas Reward". The name would suit him would be Tin Ribs,' I replied.

Often Joe would leave the dog with me for a couple of hours while he went to see his dad and brother-in-law to give them a tip-off. While he was out I felt so sorry for that animal sitting in front of the fire shivering, I gave him a roll of pig's pudding. He was ravenous – another day I gave him lumps of

157

cheese and buttered toast and meat gravy soaked in bread. Each time Hopwas was left with me I would feed him up.

The trainer saw he was putting on weight, but he couldn't understand why. Hopwas was never entered in another race. A few weeks later, I was told he had died. I was glad Joe never found out that in my ignorance I had overfed him with the wrong kind of food.

While my husband was still at the dog track, he came in contact with one of the bookmakers, Jimmy Budd. Jimmy asked Joe if he would like a part-time job collecting a few bets. As Joe loved the feel of money, this job went well for a while. On bad nights when betting was slack, Jimmy didn't want to pay much. They argued, and when Joe helped himself to his wages, that was the end of that job.

One night as we were on the way to the Elite picture house, Joe slipped into the betting shop owned by Jim and Joe Smith, to have a bet. As soon as he came out we walked towards the Elite in Soho Road. He said, 'Kate, I've had a word with Jim and Joe. They've asked me if I'd like a job collecting bets on our street corner.' As this was illegal, I was worried. 'But what if the police catch yer?' I said.

'That'll all be arranged. They'll put another dummy runner in my place, while I'm hurrying away to take in the bets. Anyway,' he added, 'I'll be workin' on commission.'

'Please yerself, if that's what yer want to do, but don't come to me to bail yer out if yer get caught!' I replied angrily.

'Come on,' he replied, 'or we'll be late for the pictures.'

Joe and I loved to see a cowboy film. But when we fumbled in the dark to find two seats, we noticed the film had already started. It wasn't until we found two empty seats in the front row, six seats away from each other, that we discovered the programme had been changed. They were showing Gracie Fields in *The Queen of Hearts*.

We were both disappointed, but watched it for about ten minutes until all of a sudden I heard Joe call out, 'Kate, come on! I ain't watchin' no mower of this bleedin' rubbish!'

I felt so embarrassed as I got up and followed him out. On the way home we had our usual quarrel, yet our arguments never lasted long. Often Joe would change the subject and make me smile with his sense of humour.

A few days later, Joe Smith called at our house to make all the necessary arrangements.

Soon he had punters come from all districts, for my husband was well known and well liked, especially amongst the women. He would often be seen with his hands in his pockets whistling some kind of ditty while waiting for bets on the street corner.

He was also known as 'The Bookie's Runner'. Often he would have pieces of toffee or a penny ready to give to some little urchin to keep a watchful eye out and warn him when he saw a 'bobby' coming.

He'd be seen standing beside a low wall, laughing and joking to some of the people who handed him the bets. Yet he was always on the alert to scale the wall and hide in someone's back entry or in their attic. When the all clear came, women would hand over their threepenny and six-penny each-way bets, and when anyone asked him to tip them a horse or a dog, he used to say, 'Do yer think I'd be standin' 'ere if I knew any certainties? Yer betta try stickin' a pin in, yer might be lucky.'

Often the police disguised themselves in slouched trilbys and long shabby raincoats, but Joe was no fool – he knew them all and was over that wall and out of sight before they ever caught him.

One morning as I walked down the street, I saw Mrs Jenks, one of our neighbours, having an argument with my husband. When she saw me she came towards me. I asked her what the trouble was, and she said, 'Yer know, Mrs Dayus, I like yower Joe, until he tries ter pay me out short. I know I can't read but I know 'ow ter reckon up to a farthin'.'

'Oh well, Mrs Jenks,' I replied pleasantly, 'we all make mistakes,' and I walked away.

My husband didn't take only threepenny, fourpenny or sixpenny bets – men came from factories all around the Jewellery Quarter with large sums of money and large bets which earned him his commission.

During the Oaks, St Leger, November Handicap and other such important races, my husband's commission more or less came to £1,500 a week. He gave me most of it to save in my bank account. We now had quite a nice little nest egg.

During the winter months we'd sit beside a roaring fire and play cards or dominoes. He taught me all kinds of games, but he was a poor loser and often grumbled when I beat him. 'Beginner's luck' he used to say, and he said red cards were unlucky for him. When he had another-coloured pack he'd say, 'Let's have a shilling on who wins.' But when I won he wanted to double up. I knew he'd win in the end, so I gave up and put my winnings in my pocket.

Some nights he would read to me from one of his cowboy books, and if I felt tired and closed my eyes he'd ask me if I'd been listening.

'Yes,' I'd reply. 'I'm only restin' my eyes.'

But when he asked me what the last chapter was about and I couldn't tell him, he'd say, 'Never mind, I'll continue tomorrow night', and put the book away

Later, Joe built himself a loft at the end of the garden for his pigeons. And after getting rid of all the builders' rubbish, he dug a garden where later I grew my own vegetables.

I felt now that I wanted to sell my business and retire. As soon as everything was sold, I had a couple of customers ask me to help them out with home work. Several weeks later Joe built me a workshop facing the back garden. Later I taught him how to do the enamelling and for several years we worked together doing outwork for T. A. Butler and R. E. V. Gomm. During those years we were very happy together.

Then one day my eldest daughter brought us the news that her husband had died tragically. She was a bundle of nerves and scared to go back to her own house. After my husband and I had made all the funeral arrangements, we talked things over and suggested she come to stay with us until such time as she could make up her mind to go back to her own home. But later she decided to sell the house and everything it contained and make her home with us.

While she was living with us, Joe and I took her on our fishing holidays in Ireland. We never left her to be lonely. He also taught her to drive the car and play bowls, and in the evening he would read to us or play cards or dominoes.

# Winnie

It was during 1955 – I remember it well. One lovely sunny afternoon, I went to Handsworth Park for a bowling match, but as I was too early I sat down on the bench outside the pavilion and waited for the other members. As I did so I thought: how different that bowling green is now – I remember it as it was years ago! Then it was always kept in tiptop condition, yet today it's been neglected; nobody seems to care when they see young lads and even grown men abusing it. It was only a few years ago that Handsworth Park had two bowling greens, some of the best greens in the Midlands. It also had one of its best teams. Some of the ladies still meet in their club house to have a roll-up, but sad to say, they don't have a team any more.

As I sat on that bench, wiping my woods and getting ready to give my partner a game, I happened to glance across the green and noticed a poorly clad elderly woman sitting on the far side. I noticed she kept staring across at me. Playing beside her were two ragged children, a boy and a girl, about four years old, pushing an empty dilapidated pram.

Just as Annie, my opponent, and I began to start our match, the children ran across the bowling green. Suddenly we saw the boy pull out his little willie, and as the little girl scratched her head and watched, he began to piddle. Suddenly, Annie cried out, 'Yer dirty little bugger! Sod off!'

Quickly the little boy fumbled to push his willie back. As the remains of the piddle ran down his legs, he began to cry.

This held up our game as the other players began to laugh, and we were getting annoyed.

'Look at *'er*, their mother!' Annie cried out. 'She ain't even botherin' about 'em, an' if they don't clear off, I'll goo over meself an' clout their ear'oles!'

'No need for that, Annie,' I replied. 'I'll take 'em over to their mum.'

Annie still stood there fuming as I held their grubby little hands. When I asked their names, the little boy replied 'Georgie'. 'An' my name's Jenny,' the little girl whispered.

As soon as I reached the woman, I asked, 'Are you their mum?'

'No,' she replied. 'I'm their grandmother.'

'Well, will you please keep the children off the green?'

As I began to walk away I heard her call out, 'Don't yer know me, Kate?'

'I'm sorry, I'm afraid I don't,' I replied. 'But if you're still here when the match is finished, I'll come back to yer.'

All at once, I heard Annie yell out, 'Cum on! Yer 'oldin' up the bloody game!'

'All right! All right!' I yelled back. 'I'm coming!'

All through our game I kept wondering who she was, and why she said I should remember her, which made me lose my concentration. I lost my game, twenty-one nil. That was the first time I ever lost with such a score, and I never lived it down. But I was pleased to know that the team had won.

I was still thinking and wondering who she was as I made my way with the players for tea, and as I looked through the window I could still see her beside the pram.

I was eager now to know who she was. I didn't wait for my tea, I took my cakes and some tea on a tray to give them. As the children stuffed the cakes into their mouths, their granny said, 'Where's yer manners?'

'Thank yer, Miss,' they managed to reply.

As soon as she had drunk the cup of tea, she said, 'Yer sure yer don't know me, Kate?'

'No, but if you'll tell me yer name, I might.'

'Me name's Winnie Nashe, we grew up together in Camden Drive.'

Suddenly I remembered. I couldn't believe my eyes. Although I remembered that she was my age, she looked old and worn. Her face was well lined and her once beautiful red hair was now turning grey.

Suddenly I flung my arms around her and kissed her. All in one breath I cried out, 'Oh Winnie, Winnie, I'm ever so happy to see you again after all these years. Where are you living now?'

'I live in one of the side streets in the All Saints district near the coal wharf.'

'Why haven't yer tried to get in touch before?'

'I didn't know where yer was livin' and it was only by talkin' ter one of me neighbours about yer, that she told me yer was playin' 'ere.'

'Well, I'm glad you found me, anyway. Come home with me and we can talk about old times,' I said.

'I'd like that, Kate, but I've gotta get back 'ome, George will be waitin' for 'is tea.'

'Who's George, yer husband?' I asked.

'No, 'e's the children's father,' she replied.

'Well, do you mind if I come home with you? I don't want to lose you again.'

'Yes, I'd like that, Kate, that's if yer don't mind the place we're livin'.'

'I ain't coming to see yer place, only you. Now stay there while I fetch me coat.'

As soon as I took the empty tray back to the club house, everyone asked who she was.

'A long-lost school friend I haven't seen for years,' I replied as I put on my coat and left.

Winnie had already put the twins in the pram and was wheeling it towards the park gates when I caught up with her. It was almost twenty minutes before we reached her home. This place, where they lived, was no better than the bug-infested hovels where we lived and played when we were children, many long years ago.

These back-to-back slums were a reminder of those forgotten years, with damp green slime clinging to the outside brickwork. There was still the familiar cry from the rag-and-bone man, and smells of urine drifting into the air from the gutters, and all kinds of rubbish littered those pavements. Today it's a different place; many of these old hovels have been pulled down to make way for tower blocks (monstrosities, I call them).

I'm no snob, for hadn't I too been dragged up in bug- and rat-infested slums? Yet as I looked around these godforsaken places these people called their homes, I felt I didn't want to be reminded of the past, or to go inside. But I couldn't hurt her feelings by making some excuse.

As Winnie pushed the old pram up a side entry, the children climbed out and joined their playmates in the yard.

As we entered the living-room, I saw an elderly thickset man in his none too clean shirtsleeves. His square chin sprouted grey stubble. When he stared at me as he sat up to the table, I noticed he had a flat nose and a cauliflower ear. I thought he must have been a prizefighter. I could see he'd had plenty to drink, for as he got up from the table he stumbled and just glared at me.

'I've brought me friend 'ome with me, George,' Winnie said.

As he made his way towards the stairs, the children ran in.

'Daddy,' the little boy cried out, 'can I cum up an' watch yer fly the pigeons?'

'Very well,' he mumbled, 'but watch yer sister don't fall down the loft this time.'

After they had gone up to the attic, Winnie closed the door.

'Is that yer daughter's husband, Winnie?' I asked.

When she nodded, I couldn't help but say, 'Whatever could she see in him – he must be old enough to be her father?' And so ugly, I thought.

'Yes,' replied Winnie. 'He was forty an' Alice was only sixteen when they got married. She 'ad ter get wed, she was four months in the family way. But 'e was good an' kind ter me an' Alice. He ain't always bin like this, an' 'e was a good-lookin' bloke until 'e went in the war, an' when 'e cum back from the army 'e looked different. It's shrapnel,' she added. 'But me daughter couldn't bear the sight of him near 'er. She used to go off with other men and leave the twins for hours, and when George found out, 'e used ter belt 'er. I tried talkin' some sense into them both and things seemed a bit better for a while – until George got a job on nights, then she'd go out an' never cum back until the early hours. Then one mornin' as I was givin' the twins their porridge, she told me she was packin' 'er things an' leavin' in a few days' time.'

'What happened about the twins – did she say she was taking them with her?' I asked.

'No, Kate, she asked me if I'd take care of them until she got settled elsewhere. I was afraid to tell George she was leadin' a bad life an' was thinkin' of leavin' us. I couldn't stand any more fights and rows. So, as long as there was peace, I kept my mouth shut. I prayed often she would cum to 'er senses. Then, to make matters worse, she told me she'd tried to 'ave an abortion, an' when I asked why, she said she didn't want another babby, because it wasn't George's. When I asked 'ow she knew it wasn't, she replied, "Well, we ain't slept together or med luv for six months an' I'm over three months now." That same night she packed 'er bags and left.'

'Where is she now?' I asked.

'I don't know, Kate, and I don't think I care any more, an' I don't believe George cares, either. He gives me wot 'e can ter look after the twins, but 'e ain't over-generous.'

'But how do you manage?'

'Well, I used ter mek peg rugs like me mum an' dad showed me. But there ain't much call for 'em today. I almost 'ave ter give 'em away.'

'But why don't you try and move away from here?'

'"Ow can I? This is my 'ome. Anyway, I can't leave me gran'children to the mercy of 'im, 'e's all right till 'e gets the booze down 'im, then I puts on their 'ats an' scarves an' we leave 'im to it. That's why I came to find you at the park.'

'I'm glad you did, Winnie. But ain't their dad got any sisters or relations that can take *their* share?'

'They don't want ter know us, but I've got plenty of kind neighbours.'

'Well, Winnie, I'll have to be going now or my Joe will be wondering where I am. But will you promise to come next

Tuesday when my husband has gone to the races and we'll have a good old natter about when we were kids?'

'I'd love that, Kate.'

'Very well, you know where I live – Uplands Road. Now promise me you'll come. Don't forget, next Tuesday.'

'I won't forget,' she replied, smiling.

As she stood on the step, several neighbours eyed me up and down, wondering who I was, but I left Winnie to explain. As I flung my arms around her again and kissed her, I called out, 'Don't forget!'

When I got home I felt very sad to think that Winnie hadn't tried to make something better of her life.

The following Tuesday, I made a large cake and laid the table with bread and jam and beef sandwiches. What they couldn't eat, I would wrap up for them to take home. About three o'clock there was a knock on the door. As soon as I opened it I asked Winnie where the twins were. She said one of her kind neighbours was looking after them.

'It don't do for 'em to 'ear too much these days,' she added.

As she came into the room I could almost see what she was thinking. As she glanced around she exclaimed, 'Wot a nice place you 'ave, Kate!'

'Never mind the place, you come and sit down and have something to eat with me.' I wasn't going to show her around the house – not because I didn't want to, but I had so much more than she had, I didn't want her to feel out of place.

But all the while we were having our tea I could see her eyes wandering around everything in the room, taking everything in. To distract her mind from her surroundings, I said, 'You're very quiet, Winnie.'

'I was thinking what I could do if I 'ad a place like this.'

'Well, it's not too late, maybe some day you will, but first you have to get out of that rut you're in.'

'How can I, with me gran'children needin' me?'

'But Winnie, you've got to think of yourself as well, and try and make a new life for yourself. Did you ever get married?' I added.

'No, Kate, I did go with a young chap but when he found out I'd had a love child, I never saw him again.'

'But you're still nice-looking, Winnie, and I'm sure you'll meet the right man one day.'

'Yes, the neighbours are always telling me that. But 'ow can I leave the twins? I luv 'em like they was me own, an' if I left 'em, who's goin' ter look after 'em?'

I knew now how she felt. I still remember it was a bitter blow for me, when I had to part with my four young children – but under very different circumstances. That was in 1931, during the Depression.

To cheer her up, I thought it best to change the subject.

'Winnie, do you remember how hungry we was when we were kids, and I raided my mum's cupboard and stole a piece of fat bacon? And as we sat on the step I told you to suck it slowly to make it last?'

'Yes, I remember. It slid down our throats before we could even chew it, an' we nearly choked.'

As soon as I saw her smile, I said, 'And do you remember when I told you about my brother Jack, stealing the pig from the farm where I went hop-picking, and how the court case ended?'

'Yes, Kate, but did 'e really steal it? It wasn't proved,' she replied.

'Yes, Winnie, he did steal it, but I don't believe he took it back to the farm; for the next few weeks we ate nothing but pork, pork and more pork. Mum even boiled the pig's trotters with all the leftover bones. We ate that much pork, we began to feel like pigs.'

She began to look more cheerful, but I still carried on talking.

'Winnie,' I began again, 'do you remember when all the kids and us two had whooping cough and our mums dosed us with castor oil, and Mrs Turner said the only thing to cure us was fumes from hot tar, and while the navvies was laying the wooden blocks between the tramlines, we were all marched down the Parade, where we had to bend over that cauldron and inhale the fumes?'

'Yes, Kate, an' we nearly choked, but we still 'ad to 'ave our dose of castor oil.'

'And still have our chests rubbed with hot tallow candles,' I replied.

'An' don't forget the old socks, Kate, soaked in camphorated oil an' fastened round our necks, when we caught mumps off the other kids in the yard.'

I felt then that I didn't want to talk about our sad experiences, but over another cup of tea Winnie began to remind me of the one night I wanted to forget.

'You remember that night, Kate,' she began, 'when we 'ad that foursome, when we was fifteen?'

'Yes,' I replied. 'But let's talk about something else.'

But she was persistent in reminding me.

'But I must tell yer, Kate, I 'aven't seen yer since that day me mum beat me an' turned me out, when I was in the family way. It took a lot of years ter forget 'Arry, but time 'eals wounds.'

'We were two silly foolish girls then, Winnie. I'd almost forgotten that night,' I replied.

'Not me, I 'ad something to remind *me*.'

'How long has it been, then?' I asked.

'Well, Alice would now be twenty, so it's gotta be over twenty years when I fell for 'er.'

As soon as I saw her tears, I quickly changed the subject: 'You'd never believe the struggle I had with that other chap, that same night. I can smile now, when I think back, but not then. He pushed me in a doorway, and when I felt his John Thomas come out I got a fright and pulled it for all I was worth, and when he screamed and rolled into the gutter I ran for my life. I thought I'd killed him. Next day I kept buying newspapers to see.'

'Did yer see 'im after?' she asked.

'Yes. But he said how sorry he was, and when he had his call-up papers, he asked me if I'd wait for him. I said I would. Some time later he sent me a birthday card with lovey-dovey words written on the back, but I never heard or saw him again.'

When it was time for Winnie to leave, I made her promise to come again and meet my second husband, Joe. She said she would. After wrapping the rest of the cake for the twins, we said the usual ta-ra.

But she never kept that promise. I wondered why. I went to her home a few days later, but as soon as she saw me she said she wished I hadn't come.

'But why?' I asked.

'Well, Kate, I feel ashamed of this place for yer ter see.'

'That's nonsense, Winnie. If you'll come and see me next week, I'll see what I can do to help you.'

She promised, but she never kept her promise. I waited two whole weeks before I called again, hoping to give her some good advice. But it was too late. When I called and found the house empty, neighbours said they'd done a moonlight flit.

Sad to say, I never saw Winnie again. Yet my childhood memories of her still live with me, and I pray and hope that one day I shall meet her.

# Trespassers Will Be Prosecuted?

Our fishing holidays in Ireland were the best of times for Joe and me. One evening after eating our supper we went across the yard to the bar, where the landlord (after a fashion) introduced us to the locals.

'These are our two boarders. An' this 'ere is Micky, Rolly, Mike, Paddy' . . . and many more.

When I saw them all staring at me, I asked the landlord why.

'They ain't used ter see any young woman in 'ere.'

'That's OK,' Joe replied. 'My wife will 'ave a Guinness and I'll 'ave a shandy.'

Later that night we got very friendly with a couple who asked us to play a foursome at cribbage. Joe and I knew the game well, and enjoyed it.

Afterwards, a couple of Irishmen asked where we'd come from and if we'd enjoyed the fishing.

'No, not yet, Paddy,' Joe replied.

''Ow's that? Plenty of big fish in these waters of ours.'

'I'm told there is,' Joe replied, 'until some little buggers started throwin' stones in the water.'

Suddenly I saw Paddy wink, and as he burst out laughing Joe said, 'It was no laughin' matter, mate.'

'No offence meant,' Paddy replied, still smiling. 'But that'd be our Mickie an' little Pat – did they try to sell yer sum of them Irish worms?'

'Yes,' Joe replied, smiling back at Paddy. 'But I'd rather 'ave 'ad Irish maggots.'

'If them's what yer want, mate, we've plenty of them – an' I mean Irish,' he added.

I was glad Joe saw the funny side; he knew it was best to be on the right side of these big burly Irishmen. But I dreaded to think what would have happened to both of us if he *had* caught one or other of those mischievous little urchins.

After Joe had bought Paddy a couple of pints of Guinness he told him the best water to fish and where there were plenty of maggots to be had free.

'Just take a bucket an' the slaughterers will fill it for yer,' Paddy said.

When Joe asked where this place was, Paddy replied, 'Yer go along over the bridge and when yer turn ter the right yer see an old wooden buildin' where they slaughter the 'orses an' goats. It's what you English call a knacker's yard. Tell Rory Paddy Magee sent yer.'

After Joe had bought him another pint, we wished everyone good night. We retired to bed, but before we went, on the way across the yard to the lavatory I met the landlady coming out.

All at once she said, 'If I was you, me dear, I wouldn't go fishin' near theea.'

'But why?' I asked. 'I always go where my 'usband goes.'

'I understand – please yourself,' she replied pleasantly. 'Good night, my dear,' she added.

As I came back across the yard I heard the landlord say to my husband, 'Yer don't wanta believe all the blarney Paddy tells yer. But yer *will* get plenty of maggots. Any'ow, whether yer fish near there, yer please yourself.'

After wishing us both good night he went to bed.

I was too tired to ask Joe any questions, and once we were undressed and in bed we were too tired even to kiss each other good night.

Next morning, we were up at the crack of dawn and ready to go. After Paddy had greeted us with the usual 'Top o' the mornin'', off we went with our paraphernalia strapped to our backs.

We walked some distance, then we saw two heavy-set Irishmen coming towards us. They had splashes of blood all over their clothes. At first glance, I thought they must have been in a fight. Later I was to find out that they were the men from the slaughterhouse, which we were heading for. When they stopped to raise their hats and to greet us with their usual 'Top o' the mornin'', Joe asked them the way and told them we'd come to do some fishing.

'You'll find it around the bend, it's the large wooden buildin' on the right,' one of them said.

'The best fishin' part of the river you'll ever find in Ireland,' the other fellow replied. 'But I wouldn't take yer missus near theea,' he added.

Joe thanked them and we hurried along. I asked, 'Why did he say I shouldn't go?'

'I suppose he thought it would smell too much. But knowin' you,' he added, 'you'll come whatever 'appens.'

I always did have an inquisitive nature, but I never realised what I was going to smell and see that morning. When we were a little distance away, we saw a large old wooden shed. Propping it up were three stout tree trunks.

As we drew nearer, I saw smoke coming out through the rafters and the stench was awful. I'd never smelt anything like it. As we got closer, we saw a big hefty fellow making his way to the doorway carrying a heavy iron cauldron full of maggots. He was dressed in an old well-worn cowgown covered with blood; his leather apron and wellington boots were covered with congealed blood too. Even his hands and arms were splashed with blood. While I was staring at him, Joe gave him Paddy's message. While they were talking, I peeped inside the shed, then wished I hadn't. The smell of burning flesh wafted out, and hanging from the low rafters was bloody wool, skin and hide; I also saw parts of dead animals strewn across a wooden bench, even on the floor.

I felt I wanted to be sick, and as I walked away I vomited into the river.

As soon as my husband saw me he sat me down on the bank.

When I had pulled myself together, I cried, 'I ain't gooin' in there!'

'But there's no other way we can get to the river, only through the slaughter'ouse, love.'

Suddenly I lost my temper. 'Joe!' I cried out angrily. 'If yer think I'm goin' through that bloody shed, with all them dead carcasses lyin' about, yer can think again!'

'But, love, it's only a few paces to the river, yer can 'old yer nose, an' if yer shut yer eyes, I'll lead yer.'

'Lead yer bloody self!' I cried out angrily. 'I'm gooin' back to the inn.'

'Very well,' he snapped. 'Please yerself. I'll see yer later.' And off he went.

After wiping my tears away, I thought: what a waste of time to go back and sit in my room on such a lovely warm day!

With my creel and rod still strapped on my back, I decided to explore the other side of the river, where I could settle down and fish.

I must have walked about two miles, around several bends of the river, until I came to a lovely stretch surrounded by trees. I looked around – not a soul was in sight, but as I glanced up at one of the trees I saw a notice: PRIVATE FISHING WATERS.

I said to myself: if anyone should come along and see me I'll say I haven't seen the notice. I undid my tackle, put one of the few worms I had left in my tin on the hook, and settled down to fish. I had the time of my life – within a couple of hours I caught four dace, three trout and a grayling. I put the trout and grayling inside the basket. The dace I threw back into the water. I had no more worms left, so I thought it was time to leave.

When I got back to the inn and entered our room, Joe stood facing me.

'Where the devil 'ave yer bin?' he cried at once.

'I went for a walk along the river.'

I wasn't going to tell him then what I had caught.

'Well, did yer catch anything?' I asked.

'Catch anything?' he cried, 'I threw in me first 'andful of maggots and they kept jumpin' up fer more. I couldn't get 'em out quick enough, great big bream they was.'

'Well, let's see 'em,' I replied anxiously.

'I threw 'em all back – I couldn't put 'em in me basket, they smelt to the high heavens.'

When he'd finished talking I said, 'Now Joe, shut yer eyes and open 'em when I tell yer.'

While his eyes were closed I opened up the basket, then showed him what I'd caught.

His eyes nearly popped out of his head. He cried, 'Wherever did yer fish them from?'

When I told him, he asked if anybody had seen me. When I told him nobody had, he made me promise not to say to the missus nor the landlord where I had been. But if they should ask, I was to say further along the river. Joe had one trout, the missus and the gaffer had one each and I had the grayling, which she cooked in wine. It was delicious.

I was surprised they never asked where I got them from, yet said that any time we brought any more she would cook them for us.

Next morning I promised to take Joe there. As soon as we arrived, he saw the notice, climbed the tree and hid it among the bushes.

While he'd gone to dig up a few worms, I got everything ready to start. As soon as he returned we stuck a worm on the end of our hooks, sat down on our fishing baskets and threw in our lines. Fifteen minutes later Joe caught a large trout, a few minutes later another, and so did I. We were very excited and about to thread another worm when we saw a well-built fellow coming through the trees towards us. We knew at once he was the water bailiff. A black-and-white sheepdog walked beside him. 'Hide them trout, quick, behind the bushes, and sit quiet, while I go on fishin',' hissed Joe.

There was no time to hide them anywhere – only in the basket. Then I sat down on it. As the man stood beside my husband, he asked, 'Have you a permit to fish here?'

'No, sir,' Joe replied.

'Did you know these are private waters?'

'No, sir, I didn't,' Joe lied.

'Surely you've got eyes to read the notice on the tree,' he replied.

'I'm sorry, but I didn't see any notice.'

As the man turned to show him, he cried, 'If I catch any more of them bloody gypsy kids around here, and up these trees again, I'll put me gun up their arse. Anyway,' he added, 'have you caught anything?'

'Only a few roach,' replied Joe.

I began to shake in my wellies when he asked to look inside the basket.

Stupidly I tried to put him off and change the subject – I began to stroke the dog. 'What a lovely coat 'e's got – what's 'is name?' I asked, smiling up at him.

'Never mind what his name is, I want yours! And I still want to look inside that basket!'

Joe, still thinking the fish were safely hidden in the bushes, said he could open it up and look with pleasure. Sure enough, as soon as he lifted the lid there was the evidence, eyes and mouth open, glaring up at him.

'Do you know these are trout?' he said.

'No, sir,' Joe lied again. 'I've never seen a trout. I thought they was roach.'

'Well,' he replied as he took out his notebook, 'you had better give me your name and address and I'll take the fish for evidence. Now you better pack up and leave.'

After we had given the bailiff our names and home address, he added, 'Next time I see you anywhere near these waters I shall confiscate your rods.'

As he took the trout and walked away he said we would hear from him later.

As soon as he'd gone and we were packing up to leave, Joe called me all the fools he could think of. 'Why dain't yer 'ide 'em in the bushes?' he snapped.

'There wasn't time. I dain't think he'd look in the basket,' I snapped. 'The dog would 'ave sniffed 'em out, any'ow.'

When he saw my tears he said he was sorry he'd lost his temper.

As soon as we arrived back at the inn, the landlord asked if we had brought some more trout. 'The missus 'as the pan on ready, Joe,' he added, rubbing his hands together.

'Sorry, mate, we dain't 'ave any luck terday.'

I noticed the landlord looked disappointed, but my husband wouldn't tell him why.

After our usual supper of bread and cheese, beef and pickles, we went across the yard to the bar, where we heard some of the locals singing.

'What's the celebration in aid of?' I asked the landlord.

'Oh, me lads always sing on Saturday nights, but ternight they're singing their numbers for you and yer missus,' he replied, turning to my husband.

I had heard Irishmen sing in our local pub at home, and when I was a child, but I'd never heard such lovely lilts and words to their songs as I did that night. As we sat among them, I thought: what a waste of talent! We saw and heard each Irishman in turn sing a number.

'Come on, Pat, let's 'ear from you.'

But when Pat began to sing 'Mountains of Mourne', the big fellow they called Mike cried out, 'Sit yerself down Pat, that's too sad, let's 'ave "Paddy McGinty's Goat".'

We laughed as we tapped our feet to the rhythm. Then it was Rolly's turn, and everybody joined in as he sang 'Abdul baba Amare'. It was a song I'd never heard before, but the words and the lilt of that tune set us all off tapping our feet. The landlord, I noticed, never objected to the noise, as several of the locals did an Irish jig.

By this time I had drunk a couple of whiskies and three Guinnesses, and was feeling merry myself. I wanted to sing a number, so I stood up and asked if I could.

I saw my husband warn me with a scowl, but I was determined to sing at least one song. But after I had finished 'Klondike Kate' and heard the loud applause, I began to sing 'That Little Shirt Me Muvver Made For Me'.

I felt so merry I could have sung all night, but when an old Irishman pulled me on to his lap I was pleased Joe came to the rescue.

'Come on, Grandad,' I heard him say. 'Enough's enough, so watch yer blood pressure.'

This caused more laughter amongst the locals.

It was now time to retire as we had to catch an early plane the next day, but Mike, the one with the lovely baritone voice, asked the landlord if he could sing one more number.

'Very well, then you must all go to yer 'omes.'

Turning to Joe, he asked, 'Do yer mind if I sing this last song for yer missus?'

Joe put his arm round me and as we sat down again the fellow gazed down at me and sang 'Kathleen Mavorneen'. Tears filled my eyes – not only because he sang it so beautifully, but I remembered back so many many years ago, when I was just sixteen, and my first husband sang it to me when we were courting.

After wishing everyone good night and saying we would come back to Ireland, we retired to our room, when Joe asked why I had wept.

'It was such a sad song and it brought back many sad memories, Joe.'

'The trouble with you, you 'ad too much to drink and . . .'

'It wasn't my fault if they asked me to 'ave one,' I replied.

'One? I counted three,' he said.

'Oh, you was jealous because I was 'avin' too much attention paid to me,' I replied as I began to weep.

Suddenly he took me in his arms and as he kissed my wet tears away he said, 'Yes, I was, love.'

As soon as we had undressed and got into bed he put his arms round me and hugged me to him. That was the last time we made love in that clean but rickety old bed. We had enjoyed our fishing holiday, and after saying our goodbyes to all the local people we promised to come back the next year.

Next morning we took the train to Dublin, where we caught the plane. After the stewardess had brought our cups of tea, I sat thinking about that water bailiff. When Joe asked me why I was quiet, I replied, 'You know, we shouldn't have given that bailiff our real address – what if we're put into prison?'

'I don't think so,' he replied, with a smile. 'He could 'ave had us arrested then and taken our rods. No, forget it, I don't want yer spoilin' yer 'oliday we've 'ad.'

As soon as we arrived home, there in the letterbox were bills and a letter with an Irish stamp on the envelope. When my husband opened it he cried, 'That crafty ol' bleeda, he must 'ave kept them trout and cooked 'em for 'imself!'

'But what's the letter say?' I asked eagerly.

'Just a warning to tell us not to fish there again. No address, an' no signature. Any'ow I still think we were lucky, Kate. It could 'ave been a real bailiff.'

The following year, 1961, we made plans to go to Ireland again, but cancelled it for two weeks at the seaside in Weymouth, where Joe had been stationed during the war. But it rained every day. It was disastrous. While we were on our way home my husband said we'd take a short cut down Rookery Road. As we walked a little way down the hill I noticed several workmen building six new houses. As soon as we got closer I thought how lovely it would be to own a newly built house where people haven't lived before.

'Joe,' I cried out at once, 'wouldn't it be nice to live in one of them?'

'Surely you ain't thinkin' of movin' again,' he replied.

'But Joe, I promise yer it'll be me last move, an' I won't get nervous any more, thinkin' about ghosts an' people committing suicide in them other 'ouses.'

'Well, wait till we get 'ome an' I'll think about it.'

'But Joe, why don't yer go an' ask one of the workmen now if they're for rent or to be sold?'

'They won't know,' he replied.

'No 'arm in askin'.'

'I've said I'll think about it,' he replied.

'All right, I'll ask meself.'

As I began to walk over loose planks of wood and piles of sand he pulled me back and made his way towards one of the workmen, who told him to enquire at the head builder's shed. After a while, he came back to tell me the houses wouldn't be finished until October but if we were interested we could go and see the estate agent. The first house in the row had a large frontage and a larger garden than the others – it was also detached.

Joe was as eager as I was now. Off we went to the address the builder had given us, and after giving him all the details we paid our deposit. In a few weeks we had everything signed, sealed and delivered, and soon we were the proud owners of 29 Rookery Road.

# Maggie

I look forward with pleasure to my visits and talks to the elderly people of my generation – also to the young people I now come in contact with in schools and libraries. Yet I find it much easier to talk to the elderly who understand about the old slums and back-to-back hovels in those Edwardian Birmingham days. It is also a tonic to me to see their faces light up as they too recall their childhood memories, and the many they had almost forgotten.

And as I begin to talk to them as they sit or lie back in their chairs, I notice that many look younger or older than me, and I thank the Good Lord that I am one of the most fortunate ones who can get about and not have to stay where these people are from day to day, year to year. I know and feel that many of them would still prefer to go back and spend the rest of their lives in their own homes – although several tell me they would rather be where they are than live with their relatives.

Many of these ladies would not be in these homes if there weren't many kind people who dedicate their services and patient care to give warmth, comfort and pleasure to the elderly.

After my talks and readings from my books, I show them the video of the old and the new Birmingham, and the story of my family and of my life.

During one of these engagements I happened to notice a small white-haired lady very cheerfully wheeling a trolley with cups of tea and cakes, handing them out to the patients. All at once she came across, smiled at me and said, 'Excuse me, but I believe I know yer, and I've bin lookin' forward ter meeting yer, and when I knew yer was comin' 'ere I was ever so pleased. I've already read yer books, that's 'ow I remembered who yer was. Would yer like a fresh cup of tea?' she added.

'Yes thanks,' I replied, smiling back.

'I'll bring you a nice china cup, not one of these thick ones,' she said.

Before she moved away I asked how she knew me, as I couldn't remember who she was. She replied, 'I used to live in Pope Street with me mum an' dad an' me sister Becky. Me name's Maggie Brown, we used ter goo ter the same school.'

Suddenly I smiled and so did she – I whispered so that no one else could hear, 'Are you the Maggie Brown the other girls called after when we had no drawers to wear?'

'Yes, an' I still remember them words,' she whispered. 'Maggie Brown's got no drawers, will yer kindly lend 'er yours.' We began to laugh.

'Now I remember you, and your sister, and how we used to get the cane for helping each other with our sums. But we never went crying to our mums like the kids do today. I only ever ran home crying to my mum once and she said I must have deserved it, and if I didn't behave myself she'd give me some more.'

'Yes,' she replied. 'We was taught discipline in them days, ter respect our teachers an' our parents.'

'When I moved up into standard four I believe you and your sister left?'

'Yes,' she replied, 'we had to do a moonlight flit and went to live in Summer Lane, near the Salutation Pub. They was worse slums than the ones we'd already left – two rooms down and one up an' the front door cum on to the edge of the pavement.'

As we were still whispering our thoughts, we noticed the warden making her way towards us. She didn't look very pleased.

'Come on, Maggie!' she called out loudly. 'You're already behind, and there's the cups to be collected and put away.'

As Maggie took my empty cup she whispered, 'That sour-faced ole bugger! I wish the other warden was back. She was kind an' understandin'. We all liked 'er, but not this one. Can yer wait an' see me after I've finished?' she called as she hurried away.

I didn't have to wait long, and when we hurried outside towards the taxi that was waiting to drive me home, I told the driver I would be catching the bus instead. Maggie and I agreed to have tea and cakes in a little tea shop round the corner. As soon as we were sitting at the table and the waitress had served us, Maggie said, 'I ain't a patient at that community 'ome, I only goo theea ter mek teas an' goo errands to 'elp the old dears, who can't 'elp themselves. But we're blest, you an' me, we *can* get about, Kate – yer don't mind me callin' yer Kate?'

'No, not at all, Maggie,' I replied as I smiled across the table to her. She was quite a chatterbox, but then so was I. Yes, she was a nice pleasant person to listen to, and I was an eager listener as we chatted together as though we were old friends.

'I don't 'ave ter do this job, Kate, but it keeps me busy an' I like it, an' the little money I earn ekes out me pension an' me social security.'

As I watched her light a cigarette, I noticed the front of her silvery-white hair was almost yellow from the nicotine smoke. As soon as she asked if *I* smoked, I replied, 'No, Maggie, I gave them up over forty years ago.'

'I wish I could, Kate, they're so expensive now. I remember when me Woodbines cost me only twopence a packet, an' a couple of matches inside free. But I am tryin' ter cut 'em down, me doctor's alwis tellin' me ter give 'em up, but I'm too long in the tooth now ter change me 'abits. Anyway,' she added, 'they 'elp ter soothe me nerves. Any'ow, 'ow did you give 'em up?'

'It was very hard at first, Maggie,' I replied. 'I used to smoke anything, whatever was cheapest. One day I happened to have a fit of coughing and thought I was going to die. It was then I threw them all into the fire – whole packets too, which I'd bought on the black market. I swore that day I'd never smoke another one. That next morning when I woke up I sat on the side of the bed gasping for one. I kept saying to myself, "No! No! I *must* break myself from 'em." A few minutes later, when I went downstairs and walked into that stale-smelling smoky room, that started me off again, wanting one all the more. If it was only one, I said, I'd promise it would be the last, and no more. I searched all the drawers and cupboards, and even turned all my pockets inside out to find a nub end. Still craving, I put the kettle on the fire to make a pot of tea, then suddenly my eyes nearly popped out of my head – staring at me from the hearth was a small nub end. Now, Maggie, you'll laugh when I tell you what I did. It was so small and dry, I stuck it on the end of a pin. I lit it and dragged on that nub till it burnt my lips. I remember that first drag tasted like nectar, until I began to cough. Again I thought I was going to die. I swore I would never smoke again.'

'But dain't yer ever get the cravin' for 'em agen?'

'Oh yes, Maggie, for days and weeks. But with perseverance, determination and willpower I managed to give them up. Also with help from a young woman I once worked with. She was always chewing on the end of a pencil, and when I asked her why she told me it stopped her from smoking, and if I ever wanted a cigarette I was to put a pencil between my lips and pretend. I did just that too, Maggie, which stopped the craving.'

'I'll try that, Kate, an' see if it'll 'elp.'

We both enjoyed chatting to each other, and as she ordered another two cups of tea, I went on to say, 'One day, as I walked along the Parade, I came towards a tobacconist's shop on the corner of Congreve Street, and in the window, surrounded by thousands of cigarettes, sat an old man rolling them on a small hand machine. As soon as I felt the craving come back I walked quickly past, took out me pencil and as I put it to my lips and pretended to puff away the imaginary smoke, I saw several people stop and stare. They must have thought I was crazy! But I didn't care – I knew I was cured. Now that's another habit I have – whenever I'm concentrating

I always put my pen to my lips, but it's the better habit of the two.'

As I got up to go after tea, she said, 'Would yer like ter come ter my 'ome one afternoon an' 'ave tea? I'd luv ter tell yer about my young life.'

As soon as I promised, she wrote down her address and I gave her my phone number to ring me when it was convenient. We kissed each other, then waved as she got on the bus. As it was a lovely warm afternoon, on my way home I strolled through the park, where I saw two young girls about ten years old sitting on the grass, playing a guessing game with a stone held behind their backs. And as I stood for a few seconds to watch, I remembered my young days when I used to sit on the pavement with my brother Frankie and other boys playing at marbles and five stones. As I stooped down to watch, I asked, 'Do you ever play five stones?'

'What's them?' the little girl asked.

'Would you like me to show you?'

When they nodded, I picked up five very small stones from the gravel path, and after wiping the dust from them I sat down beside them and showed them how to play. As soon as I could see they had got the idea of the game, I left, but when I looked back I was pleased to see that other children were sitting round to watch. Sad to say, we don't see many children play the games we did when we were young. There was skipping with our mothers' washing lines, Whip and Tops, marbles, hopscotch, and many other games, which cost little or nothing in those days but amused us and kept us out of mischief.

# Maggie and Harry

A few days later I had a phone call from Maggie asking me to come to her home to tea on the following Monday, and she would meet me at the King's Standing bus terminus.

I looked forward to seeing her again, and to more talks about those old days. That Monday as I waited in that bus queue, it started to rain heavily. There was no shelter anywhere. Even if there had been, I didn't want to miss my turn in the queue.

When the bus came I noticed it was full, and it drove on. Everybody started to grumble and swear, and I was in two minds whether to go back home, yet I didn't want to disappoint Maggie. So I stayed grumbling with the rest until the next bus came fifteen minutes later, and I was lucky to find standing room. As soon as I arrived at the terminus, I saw Maggie waving to me from the shelter.

'I'm sorry I'm late, but the first bus was full,' I said.

'Never mind,' she replied, opening up her umbrella for me to share. Then as she took my arm we hurried to a nearby cul-de-sac, where I saw six houses each side of a grass verge. I noticed how clean and well kept they were. As Maggie put the key into the lock, and closed her umbrella, I began to wipe my feet on the hallway mat, just as two neighbours hurrying past called out 'Good afternoon' to her.

'I've got some good, kind neighbours,' she said. 'They always keep an eye on me 'ouse or call to see if I want anythink.'

'Sounds like the old times,' I replied.

'Yes, Kate, but yer can't leave yer door unlocked now like we used to, too many break-ins around here.'

'Yes, I've had my home broken into twice, in the daytime too, and Bobby, my dog, beaten up. If ever I'd have caught

186

them, Maggie, I believe I would have killed 'em, whether I was wrong or right,' I replied bitterly.

'We 'ad nothing to fear, Kate, not in that way – I suppose because we 'ad nothing worth pinchin' anyway,' she added. 'Let me 'ave yer wet 'at an' coat.'

As I handed them to her she made me sit by the fire and take off my wet shoes and stockings. After giving me a towel she handed me a pair of her warm slippers. I sat by that welcome fire with my feet resting on that shining brass fender and looked around the room, while she went into the kitchen to make some tea.

The table was laid with a white lace tablecloth and home-made sandwiches, cakes and bread and butter. Everything looked well worn but homely, clean and highly polished, even the black-leaded range you could see your face in.

As soon as she came in from the kitchen with the teapot and saw me gazing around, she asked, 'Do yer like me place, Kate?'

'Yes,' I replied. 'How long have you lived here?'

'Since we was bombed out in Summer Lane.'

We had our first cup of tea, then drew our chairs up to the table. As we sat eating, we often stopped to talk.

'When I read your books,' she began, 'I remembered all those streets and dark alleyways and some of the people who lived there near Pope Street where we lived. An' do you remember an old pub called the Lion an' the Lamb?'

'Yes,' I replied. 'When it closed down it was taken over by the Salvation Army, and my sister-in-law and her young daughter dished out to us poor free basins and jugs of stew and a piece of bread.'

'Was that your sister-in-law? I remember 'er ever so well, 'er name was Rose. She was alwis kind to the poor unfortunates, an' everyone liked Rose an' spoke well of 'er. She lived in Pope Street opposite Morton Street near us.'

'She was married to my brother Jack. Her real name was Rhoda, but everybody called her Rose. They both gave me away in 1921 at my wedding at Saint Thomas's Church in Bath Row, but we don't see any of them old-fashioned weddings any more, where all the neighbours celebrated too, and had the old gramophone in the yard or booked the hurdy-gurdy man, so everybody could have a knees-up to the tune from the old barrel organ.'

'Yes, Kate, them were some of the happy times. But I've known several young girls who ran away from 'ome who was pregnant an' gave birth to babbies born out of wedlock. My sister Becky was one of those unfortunates, but me mum put 'er pride in 'er pocket an' ignored the neighbours' gossip, an' between me an' me mum we managed to rear that lovely little girl until she died with whoopin' cough, an' she was only three, Kate. Our Becky was always out gooin' ter dance 'alls an' when she come 'ome late, me dad would be waitin' with 'is leather belt. But that seemed to 'arden 'er all the more an' she ran away from 'ome. The next time we saw 'er she was standin' by the graveside at me dad's funeral, all painted an' dolled up, but as soon as she saw all the neighbours staring at 'er an' whispering to each other, she left. We never saw 'er agen, until me mum was dying with that deadly disease, consumption.'

'Is your sister alive now?' I asked.

'Yes, she lives not far from 'ere, but since I buried me mum I don't ever wish ter speak to 'er again,' replied Maggie bitterly. 'She's livin' with a married man now old enough ter be 'er grandad, an' 'e knocks 'er about, so I 'ear from neighbours. She also 'as a son, my nephew, who is now 'appily married with a lovely wife an' three young children. 'E never goes ter visit his mother, yet 'e always cums ter see me every Saturday afternoon when there's a football match. 'E's rough an' ready but 'e's gotta 'eart of gold.' But when she spoke of her sister I noticed she became very bitter.

'Maggie,' I said. 'You shouldn't feel too badly towards your sister. Maybe if she hadn't fallen for that child, she might have been a different person. Women like us were brought up in squalor and ignorance, but children today are taught the facts of life and know what life is all about.'

\* \* \*

When I was ready to go, Maggie seemed reluctant for me to leave. Then there was a knock at the door and in walked a tall, handsome young man in shabby dark-blue overalls.

''Ello, 'Arry!' Maggie cried, as she reached up to kiss him. Turning to me, she said, 'This is me nephew, Kate, and 'Arry, this is me friend I used ter goo ter school with, the lady who wrote them books yer bought me.'

'I'm very pleased ter meet yer, Mrs Dayus. I've 'eard such a lot about yer an' I've read yer books, me an' me wife, an' when me daughters grow up they too will 'ave ter read 'em.'

'What brings yer 'ere today, 'Arry?' asked Maggie.

'Will yer loan me a couple of quid till termorra, yer see I've cum without me wallet, an' I wanta goo ter me club straight from work.'

As she handed him the two pounds he kissed her and said he'd call the next day.

After shaking my hand he said, 'Keep up the good work, dear.'

After closing the door behind him, Maggie said, 'E's a good lad, always pays me back, an' although I'm only 'is auntie, 'e always brings me flowers on Mother's Day, an' other times 'e does odd jobs for me. I've only gotta ask.'

I gave her my address and phone number again and told her to ring me when it was convenient.

She saw me to the bus, then we waved each other goodbye.

A few days later I heard from her – she was already in town shopping and would I meet her outside the Kardomah Café?

When we met she said she was sorry to have kept me waiting but she had been kept waiting at the shops.

'Never mind, Maggie,' I replied, 'you're here now, so let's finish our coffee and catch the bus.'

Seeing the bus coming we hurried to catch it, and luckily the kind driver waited for us.

As soon as we got off the bus and arrived at my house, I said I'd already got the table laid for tea. As we walked up the front-garden path she said, 'You've got a nice 'ouse, Kate, do yer live 'ere all alone?'

'No, my eldest daughter and her husband live with me. Anyway they're away on holiday at the moment, and I'm happy to have the house to myself.'

When she asked how long I had lived in Handsworth, I told her that Joe and I had bought the house in 1961. 'But Handsworth's not like it used to be when we first came to live here. There was always those lovely old small familiar shops, where the people served you across the counter and always found time to have a friendly chat while measuring and weighing whatever you asked for. But we don't get that today. Food's already wrapped and your money taken and you never know what you've really bought until you unwrap it. It's the attitude you get from some of these supermarkets: "Take it or leave it".'

'Yes, Kate, I know wot yer mean – give me the old friendly corner shops any time.'

As we sat at the table and began our tea, I said, 'But I wouldn't like to see those poverty days again.'

'Nor me, Kate, nor live in them back-ter-back slums agen. It was a good thing in one way that Summer Lane came under the bombing, otherwise I think I would still be there terday. Yet it's sad when yer think of all them people who were killed. Did yer ever know Summer Lane, Kate?' she added.

'No, but I'd heard of it and was warned not to go near it when I was a kid.'

All at once we both began to laugh like a couple of teenagers, then Maggie cried, 'It was a street where men threw corks at each other with the bottles on the end. Police often paraded four abreast, an' many a man was frogmarched ter Kenyon Street Police Station for disturbin' the peace, women too dragged out of the pub. Some women were afraid of no man – often on Saturday nights, even Sunday dinner-time, you'd see an' 'ear a man an' wife fightin' over their kids, even over other people's cats an' dogs.'

'Talking about cats, Maggie, I remember a woman who lived in the end house in our yard – her name was Mrs Taylor, she had several cats and when they had kittens she used to drown them in the maiding tub, under the tap. And when the corporation men came she used to cover 'em over with ashes and hide them in the dustbin. Then our dry closets were demolished and we had the flush ones, but still the same wooden seats. Then one day we saw Mrs Bumpham come out of the end closet with her drawers hanging down over her boots, screaming her head off, shouting she'd heard a baby cryin' down in the basin. Somebody fetched the police and when they investigated they found it was another place where Mrs Taylor drowned her kittens. Do you know, Maggie, how superstitious people were in them times? Nobody would use that closet in case one came up and clawed at their bum. It was nailed up until the day Mrs Taylor died.'

'Are you superstitious, Kate?' she asked.

'Yes, I believe I am in many ways.'

'So am I,' replied Maggie, 'especially when I tek a walk in the cemetery – I never walk on the grass in case I walk on somebody's grave. I'm told it's bad luck. An' the people cum an' 'aunt yer.'

'I don't believe that one, Maggie,' I said, smiling.

'I do, Kate; there was a neighbour of ours who lived in Summer Lane, she an' 'er husband were alwis fightin' an' when 'e died she said she wanted 'im cremated ter mek sure 'e was dead. Yet people couldn't understand why she kept 'is ashes in a vase on the kitchen shelf. When the neighbours found out and told 'er it was bad luck, she wouldn't believe 'em until a few nights later she began to 'ave nightmares. Somebody told 'er if she got rid of 'is ashes the nightmares would goo. A few days later, when we saw 'er sling 'is ashes through the winda, me nor none of our neighbours would walk on that part of the pavement until the rain cum an' washed 'im away. She's also cum ter live in King's Standin' not far from 'ere. Yer see there's no pawnshops now, near 'ere, but there used ter be a special bus laid on every Monday mornin', called the Jenny Brigton Bus, for these women ter tek their bundle of clothes or whatever, ter the Jenny Brigton's pawnshop in Summer Lane.'

'Yes, Maggie,' I replied, 'I was glad when *I* could find

something to pawn, it was better than going to the loan sharks.'

We laughed and cried as we talked about the many things that happened those long years ago. And when she asked me why I didn't talk the lingo like the Brummies, I replied, 'I do – you should hear me when I lose me temper, Maggie!'

I also told her about the different boyfriends I had, and how I came to educate myself.

'I remember when I was about twelve I became one of my teacher's favourites. Her name was Miss Frost. She tried hard to teach me how to pronounce words properly, and when I did, all the kids in our street used to make fun of me. When I was fourteen and left school, I was determined to teach myself to talk better. It was not until I started work that I began to listen to the office girls and try to pronounce words as they did. And when I was about fifteen, still ignorant and innocent, I met a boy from the office. We often went for walks together, he too spoke very nicely, yet I could never break myself of the Brummie lingo. Then, one Sunday afternoon, as we strolled through the park, he stopped to put his arm round me and kiss me. Although I liked that sensation, Maggie, I was scared of what it might lead to. As I pushed him away I cried out, "Goo away! I ain't one of yer sort yer can tek yer way with, wot werks in yer office." Do you know, Maggie, after he said he was sorry, I still felt I wanted him to take me in his arms and kiss me, really passionately. But being dragged up and not knowing the facts of life, I was scared. Then one day, as we strolled through that same park, he began to say I was a nice girl and if I would let him teach me to speak properly I could go places; he also said he'd bring a dictionary and teach me. I didn't even know what a dictionary was until he explained. But when he told me he'd like to take me to his home to meet his parents, but I had to learn to pronounce my words properly, I suddenly felt ashamed and embarrassed. I lost my temper and slapped his face as hard as I could and ran off. He still pestered me to go out with him, but after the girls I worked with began to talk and get the wrong ideas about us, I left.

But I always remembered his words, and that he wanted to educate me. Then one day, a few weeks later, I did buy a dictionary. Although it seemed all Chinese to me I studied it hard, and when I did try to speak properly my brothers and sisters made fun of me and my mum said talking that way would be the ruination of me, and if any time she saw it she would put it on the fire. So I had to hide it away under the floorboards. And do you know how I began to learn, Maggie? Apart from listening to other people's conversations, I used to sit for hours on our wooden-seated closets and study and talk to myself, until somebody banged on the door and asked how long I was going to be. Then I'd quickly push the diary down inside my passion-killers.'

'Passion-killers? Wot are them?' Maggie asked at once.

'That's what the lads used to call our baggy bloomers,' I replied, smiling.

'Oh yes, I remember now, they was fleecy-lined with 'lastic round the legs!'

After we had talked some more about life, Maggie said she would have to be going before it got dark. And as she put on her hat and coat, she said, 'I could tell yer stories, Kate, that would mek yer 'air curl. P'raps when I cum agen, but I must 'urry now, I don't like ter goo under them underpasses, yo 'ear of too many muggin's.'

I offered to call a taxi for her, but she said she'd left a note for her nephew to say when she would be back. Just as we went along the hall and opened the front door, I saw her nephew get out of his car. As soon as she saw him she cried, 'Wot brings yer 'ere? I left yer a note ter say I'd be 'ome by five o'clock.'

'That's OK, Auntie, I thought I'd pick yer up any'ow, get in.'

She kissed and thanked me and got into the car. Her nephew said she looked forward to seeing me, but he hoped she hadn't talked me to death.

'No, she can come any time, we both enjoyed our reminiscences.'

As I waved them both goodbye, I felt so alone. So I went

indoors, put Bobby's lead on and took him for his usual walk before it got too dark.

I couldn't understand why Maggie never kept her promise to visit me that following week. I had a premonition that something was wrong when I saw her nephew at the door. As soon as I called him in, he sat down and wept. When I asked what was wrong, he managed to tell me that his Auntie Maggie had been standing on a chair, hanging up some curtains, and had fallen off.

'I don't know 'ow long she'd been lyin' on the floor, but one of the neighbours saw 'er through the winda, an' phoned me at work. She was unconscious. I dain't know wot ter do, I couldn't wait for the ambulance, so I managed to get 'er in the car and drove to the hospital. The doctors said she'd broken 'er arm in two places an' she 'ad a broken 'ip.'

When I asked if I could go and visit, he said she had died the following day.

'If only she had waited an' asked me to 'ang 'em. But she was so independent, always sayin' "If yer want things done right, do 'em yerself".' As he sobbed, he managed to say, 'I shall miss 'er so much, Mrs Dayus. She was betta than a mother ter me, she brought me up like a son when my mother left me ter roam the streets.'

I was very upset too, I didn't know what to say to comfort him. So I made him a cup of strong coffee and after pulling himself together and wiping away his tears, he asked if I would like to see her when they brought her home in her coffin.

'I'm sorry, Harry,' I said at once, 'but I would rather remember Maggie as I last saw her.'

'I understand,' he replied. 'But p'raps yer would like ter cum ter the service?'

'Yes, I'll do that, Harry. Just phone and tell me when.'

A few days later I bought a wreath and went to the service, and as I stood by the graveside I saw Harry and his wife, also several neighbours weeping. I looked among the faces to see if I could see Maggie's sister Becky. Although I'd never met her I expected she might be among the crowd. And as I glanced around again, I saw an old woman dressed in a shabby black coat and straw hat, standing well back from the graveside and weeping. I could tell she was Harry's mother – their features were almost identical. Yet no one spoke to her or went near her. Then as soon as the coffin was lowered into the grave, I watched as Maggie's sister walked away.

As soon as I arrived home, I broke down and wept. I felt I had lost a very dear friend and companion.

# Fred

When I married Joe Dayus in 1946, it was mainly for companionship. Although he had a wonderful sense of humour, in later years he became very moody, but I didn't have to be dependent on his moods. Often when we had sharp words over money matters, I got the feeling that he wished I wasn't so independent and would ask his advice on various matters. But over the years I had become too hardened in my ways to humble myself or to ask anyone's advice. I also realised that he was becoming very jealous of anyone talking to me. He would ask, 'What did they say? And who were they?' And when I bought a new dress he would say, 'I don't know why yer keep buyin' new frocks for, wastin' yer money.' Maybe I was a bit extravagant at times.

Whenever Joe took me to his fishing club and any of his friends looked at me, I could always feel his eyes on me.

Then, one day, one of his fishing mates called. I was surprised when I answered the door and saw it was a fellow that had been sweet on me some years before I was married.

'Hello, Kate, long time no see, remember me?'

'Yes,' I replied. 'What do you want?' I asked him nervously.

Although I had nothing to be ashamed of, I was afraid that if Joe knew he was one of my cast-offs, there'd be more questions and more quarrels.

When he asked if Joe was in, I invited him in. Joe was up at the top of the garden, feeding his pigeons. As soon as I went to the back door to call him, I felt Fred come too near me for comfort. I pushed him away, hoping my husband hadn't seen him, but I could see by the way he spoke he was annoyed.

# Fred

'What brings you here? I told yer I'd meet yer at the club.'

'I was passing, I thought I'd call and look at yer birds.'

'How long have yer been interested in pigeons?' he asked sharply.

'Me dad used to have them to train, years ago.'

I could see by the look on my husband's face that he didn't believe a word. 'Well, come on then, Fred,' he replied as he quickly grabbed his hat and coat, and after giving me orders to feed the rest of his birds and lock them up, he gave me a quick peck on the cheek and they were gone.

Fred didn't call again until a few weeks later. He must have known I was alone, for in his hand was a large box of chocolates. I didn't like to refuse, or to hurt his feelings. I thanked him and told him not to call again when my husband wasn't at home, as he was very jealous of anyone calling to see me.

'No harm done, Kate. I happened to win 'em an' my wife can't eat chocolates, so I thought of you. Anyway, I expect I'll be seeing you at the club.'

'Thank you, Fred,' I replied nervously as I placed the box on the table, hoping Joe wouldn't walk in at the same time.

After Fred had gone, as I picked up the two-pound box, my mouth began to water. I wanted to open them, but I was afraid Joe would come home unexpectedly and ask questions, so I hid them away. Later I thought: what if he should find them? I didn't want to make excuses to avoid more quarrels. The next day I gave them to the woman next door to share amongst her children. I told her they had been won in a raffle and I couldn't eat them.

The following week Fred came again with a beautiful bunch of carnations. I had always loved flowers, so I couldn't refuse them – and I had no intention of giving these away. 'Why should I?' I thought to myself. As I arranged them in a vase of water, we chatted for about ten minutes. He spoke about his wife and his allotments and the flowers he grew. When I asked him if he'd stay and have a cup of tea he said he was pushed for time, but if I didn't mind he'd call another day. I thanked him again for the flowers and as soon as he left I knew that when Joe saw them he would ask me where they came from. I wasn't going to lie, and I didn't want to give them away.

Sure enough, as soon as he came through the door the first thing he saw on the table were the flowers. I was glad to see he was in a good mood. 'Them are beautiful carnations, where did yer buy 'em from?'

'I didn't,' I replied. 'Fred brought 'em for me from his allotment.'

I wondered if he knew about the chocolates when he suddenly became very angry: 'This has gotta stop! I ain't havin' him bringin' yer flowers or anythin' else – if yer want any it's up ter me ter buy 'em fer yer!'

I was afraid. I'd never seen him so angry. Suddenly he snatched the flowers from the vase and hurried out of the front door with them in his hand.

I don't know what he did with them, but we never spoke to each other for the rest of that day.

The following day he came home all smiles, carrying a large bunch of red roses. I glared at him as I said, 'If yer think that yer can buy me over by bringing flowers, you've time ter think agen.'

I didn't speak to him again for days. It was only that I felt sorry for him when he developed a bad cold. But in the meantime I felt sad to see those lovely roses left drooping beside the sink. Then as I put the kettle on the fire to make some tea I saw him put them into a vase of water, and each morning when he came downstairs the first thing he did was to change the water. I never knew what became of those lovely carnations, but Fred never called at my house again, and if I ever saw him out shopping with his wife I would avoid him.

A few weeks later, I happened to see him going towards the club. As soon as I caught up with him, I asked why he never came to see me again.

'I thought it best not to call again, Kate, after Joe made such a fuss about those flowers I brought you. We nearly came to blows the way he carried on. Bad-tempered bugger,' he added.

'What did he do with the flowers?' I asked.

'He gave 'em to the barmaid.'

'I'm sorry, Fred, about the quarrel, but Joe hasn't been well lately and he gets so short-tempered and irritable at times.'

'Yes, Kate, we've all noticed that even when he's playing snooker and he loses, he throws his cue down on the floor. He was never a bad loser until these last few weeks. Anyway, I'm sorry to say the gaffer here will refuse him if he don't change. But the incident is forgotten as far as I'm concerned.'

'Thank you, Fred. I'll try and have a talk to him.'

But I knew it would be hopeless. As soon as I got home, I found Joe fast asleep in his armchair. He was also now a chain smoker, and often complained of a pain in his chest. But no matter how much I talked to him and even nagged him at times, it made no difference. I began to worry when he refused to see the doctor.

One day, whilst he was in the garden flying his birds, I cleaned and dusted the front room where he always sat. I also gave an extra polish to the hearth, which was often covered with cigarette ash. After putting a lump of coal on the fire, I left to do some shopping. When I arrived back the room reeked of stale smoke and more nub ends were strewn in the hearth. As I opened the window, Joe came in.

'What yer wanta open that bloody winda for?' he bawled. 'Want me ter catch me death?'

Suddenly I lost my patience. 'It ain't fresh air that's goin' ter kill yer, it'll be them bloody fags yer keep smokin'! An' look at me hearth agen!'

I felt sorry that I'd lost my temper when he replied, 'Yer won't have me here much longer to nag when I ain't here ter make yer a mess.'

I knew he wasn't in good health, but through all these years I still remember those words.

* * *

A couple of days after I was on to him again, to see the doctor about his cough. My daughter Jean visited us with my young granddaughter Chrissie (whom we often called 'Cookie'), who was about eight years old. As soon as Joe saw her he said, 'Would you like to play a game of dominoes, Cookie?'

'Yes, please, Grandad Dayus.'

'I don't like yer callin' me Grandad, I ain't yer real grandad, so yer can call me Uncle Joe.'

'OK, Uncle Joe,' she replied, smiling up at him.

She didn't tell him she already knew how to play, and when he drew up the coffee table by the fire he shuffled the dominoes and began to play seriously.

Jean and I left them to sit and play while we went into the kitchen to talk and make a cup of tea. Whilst we were there, Chrissie won the first two games. 'Beginner's luck' we heard Joe say. As we watched, she also won the next. But when she won the fourth game, he lost his temper and as he tipped the table up, the dominoes fell into the hearth. I had to rescue the double six from the fire. My young granddaughter was so scared, she never came again while Joe was there. I felt so ashamed and embarrassed. I still have those dominoes, with the double six which is all scorched.

As the days went by he became worse, his temper frayed and he became very irritable. At times he would say things that made me laugh, but you knew you could laugh with him but never at him.

Some days he was better than others, but little did I think I was going to be a widow for the second time so soon.

One night, as we lay in bed, he sat up fighting for his breath. I ran downstairs and phoned for the doctor. As soon as he came and examined Joe's chest, he said he would have to be moved to the hospital. Joe refused, but the doctor was adamant. 'I'm not asking you, I'm telling you!' he snapped. 'You've had a bad heart attack!'

The ambulance came and he was in St Chad's Hospital for two weeks. As soon as he came back home he began to smoke worse than before. When I had to call the doctor in again, and told him about the coughing and smoking, he called me into the hall and told me Joe had an enlarged heart and a thrombosis. There was nothing more he could do, he said, only get him to take his tablets regularly. Often he refused to take them, he said they made him feel worse. A few days later he was taken to Dudley Road Hospital. As soon as he was discharged he took up bowling again at his club.

As I was captain of the bowling team, my daughter and I had to go to Manchester to play an away match. My husband was sorry he couldn't come with us, as he had promised his club members to join their team on the same day. But he said he would have our teas ready for us when we came back.

During that afternoon I had a premonition that something was going to happen. As soon as I arrived home I received the sad news that my husband had died whilst playing on the bowling green.

I thought I would never get over my loss, but I pulled myself together and after the funeral I still carried on with my enamelling at home, also going to my bowling matches.

After a few months my daughter married again, but bowling trips, Christmas and holidays were never the same for me again.

Although Joe died many years ago, I still miss him and I think only of the happy times we had together. Yet I am not lonely any more – I have my meetings and visits to the elderly, and visits from my family. But life doesn't seem the same without a partner to confide in and share your troubles with. Although my Joe had many faults I still loved him and understood him, and often wish he were here today for us to grow old together. Now it's too late. But that's life.